Fishes of the year

'The Highlights'

Ulrich Glaser sen.

Acknowledgements

Photos:

We would like to thank the following specialists, companies, breeders and hobbyists for their advice and kindly letting us use their slides. We also thank all those we might have forgotten.

Jonathan Amitava Rao Dieter Bork
Hans Georg Evers   Janet Gan
Jürgen Glaser   Hans J. Mayland
Ralf Paul   Uwe Römer
Frank Schäfer   Erwin Schraml
Dr. Lothar Seegers   Ingo Seidel
Frank Teigler   Uwe Werner
Frank Warzel

Aquarium Glaser GmbH,
for providing beautiful fish for our photographers
from their weekly imports

amtra - **Aquaristik GmbH,**
for providing furnished aquaria
and equipment for testing

Veterinary consultant:
Dr. med. vet. Markus Biffar,
veterinarian, fish specialist

Liability:

Further useful tips about care and maintenance can be found every six weeks in AQUALOGnews, the unique newspaper for all friends of the hobby.

Read, for example, the latest breeding reports in the news. It is available in German or English and can be obtained at your local pet shop or subscribed to at the publisher.

Order your free specimen copy!

Die Deutsche Bibliothek - CIP-Einheitsaufnahme

AQUALOG: *Special* - **Serie Ratgeber**
Mörfelden-Walldorf: A.C.S.
Fishes of the year - The Highlights - 1998

Fishes of the year - The Highlights
Ulrich Glaser sen. - Mörfelden-Walldorf: A.C.S.
(Aqualog)

ISBN 3 - 931702 - 69 - 3
NE: Glaser, Ulrich sen.

© **Copyright by:**   Verlag A.C.S. GmbH
                        Rothwiesenring 5
                        D-64546 Mörfelden-Walldorf
                        Germany

Author:
Ulrich Glaser sen.
Scientific consultant:
Dipl. Biologe Frank Schäfer
Translation:
Monika Schäfer M.A./Mary Bailey
Index and organisation:
Wolfgang Glaser
Editor:
Dipl. Biologe Frank Schäfer
Cover Layout:
Gabriele Geiß, Büro für Grafik, Frankfurt a.M.

Print, typesetting, processing:
Lithographics: Verlag A.C.S.
Prepress/Photo processing/Layout:
Dipl. Wirt. Ing. (FH) Michael Blügel
Print: Giese-Druck, Offenbach
Printed on EURO ART,
100 % chlorine free paper

Editors adress:
Verlag A.C.S. GmbH
Liebigstraße 1
D-63110 Rodgau
Fax: +49 (0) 6106 - 644692
E-mail: acs@aqualog.de
http://www.aqualog.de

PRINTED IN GERMANY

Cover Photos:
Apistogramma panduro - D. Bork
L-204 *Panaque* spec. - I. Seidel
Corydoras fowleri - E.Schraml/Archiv A.C.S.
Photo on page 2/3:
Apistogramma panduro - D. Bork

Contents

The Author

Ulrich Glaser sen.

There is not much to say about his person, really. He not one of those enthusiasts who got involved in the hobby from early age on. He spend his youth (Mr. Glaser was born in 1937) trying to get through the awful times following WW II as best as he could. Of course, his mother was concerned with simply getting herself and her family through these times of poverty and hunger and there was neither time nor opportunity to get interested in any kind of 'hobby'. Taking up studies at university was simply impossible.

Owing to the circumstances, Ulrich Glaser's first contact with the aquarium hobby was finally made in a pet shop. There, he learned absolutely anything one needs to know about keeping ornamental fish, from cleaning tanks to breeding rare and precious species. Today, he is looking back on years and years of aquarium and fish tending - a very experienced enthusiast he is indeed.

After having managed several ornamental fish wholesale companies, he founded his own business, together with his wife and his two oldest children, in 1984: Aquarium Glaser which is today Europe's biggest ornamental fish import/export company and, being now managed by his daughter, has gained a lot of respect in the ornamental fish business. A few years later, a second branch developed from the fish wholesale company: amtra-Aquaristik, managed by his older son. amtra-Aquaristik produces the well-known amtra products which are sold world-wide.

Still being involved in the import/export business, Ulrich Glaser often found it extremely difficult, if not impossible to identify newly imported fishes - there simply was no useful identification literature available. Out of this unsatisfactory situation the idea developed to start an identification catalogue series: the AQUALOG was born.

In 1995, Ulrich Glaser founded Verlag A.C.S., together with his younger son. The biologist Frank Schäfer, taking over the task of scientific editor, completed the AQUALOG team.

This team has set itself the goal to catalogue all known ornamental fishes of the world and publish reference books with high-quality, multi-coloured photographs. There are - approximately - 40,000 fish species and we have a long way to go if our task is to be realised. But we think, friends of the hobby and specialists alike will appreciate our work.

In order to keep the AQUALOG series handy and easily comprehensible, each book treats one group or genus of fishes. The most beautiful and popular species are shown on an extra poster and introduced in this Special series. All species belonging to each group or genus, including all varieties and breeding forms, are presented in the respective AQUALOG book.

All AQUALOGs can be supplemented which means that pictures of newly discovered or bred fishes can be attached on the free pages in the back part of the book. This way, the owner of an AQUALOG can - easily and cheaply - keep the catalogue up-to-date for years and years.

Also, we developed a genuine code-number-system that labels every single fish species and its varieties with an individual code-number. The fish keeps this number even if some day its name is changed. The individual code-number makes every fish absolutely distinctive and internationally communicable, leaving language barriers behind.

Wolfgang Glaser

Preface

The AQUALOG advisory special series provides easily comprehensible information, presenting fishes of certain group in many beautiful pictures, easy text and useful drawings.

All aquarists and especially beginners who start to get involved with the wonderful hobby, will find a lot of useful advice regarding care, maintenance and breeding.

The advisory specials are written by experienced specialists who love to tell you all about the tips and tricks one can learn when spending many years keeping and breeding ornamental fishes.

This advisory special no. 7 is focused on ornamental fishes that are marketed and have never before been seen in the aquarium hobby.

Many ornamental fishes are introduced that have either been newly bred or discovered, i.e. have not yet found their entry into the available specialist literature. Others that had been considered to be 'lost' for a very long time and are now 're-discovered' are also included - we owe a huge thanks to those importers and breeders whose efforts made this possible.

Further, species are introduced that are indeed known in the hobby but deserve - in my opinion - extra attention because they are the prize winners of the 98 AQUARAMA in Singapore.

We feel that these fishes should not be forgotten in a special on the "Fishes of the Year"!

Besides the pictures included in the text, we present the 64 most beautiful and popular species on the accompanying poster in fantastic high-quality photos.

The captions not only provide each fish's scientific name but also its code-number and the 'common name' used in the trade.

Further, the captions include care instructions and the most important characteristics of the respective fish in form of catchy symbols so that you don't have to re-read the text in order to get the basic information about a certain fish. The explanation of the symbols is on page 48 of this book.

We are especially grateful to all photographers and all others who were involved in the making of this book and who provided their knowledge.

We hope you enjoy reading this book and that it gives you an interesting overview of the beautiful 1998 "novelties".

Your AQUALOG team

Wolfgang Glaser

Basics:
Are there still 'new' species being discovered?

We 'modern beings' live in the so-called "space age", a time marked by incredible new technologies. The fact that man travels in space and walks on the moon suggests that the earth holds no secrets any more and that everything has been discovered.

Well - in fishes, we learn that, indeed, the time of new discoveries is far from over. This is partly due to the fact that rivers and lakes can hardly be 'scanned' completely in order to know how many species actually are do live in a certain biotope.

It might sound unbelievable, but there are many regions on this planet where nobody ever has looked for fishes. This might be due to the fact that many biotopes, especially in the tropical regions, are almost completely inaccessible for human beings. So, the efforts made by aquarists and scientists to discover new species for the aquarium hobby cannot be appreciated too much, as they are often tiresome and even dangerous.

If you look at a map of the earth and the huge freshwater areas of South America, Africa, Asia and Australia, you might get an idea of how many undiscovered species are still 'waiting' there to be found. Any aquarist who has ever travelled to such an area and has seen these enormous waters, sometimes appearing as inland seas, sometimes as labyrinths of rivers and streams, will know that very often it is simply impossible to get access to the biotope he would like to examine.

In the tropics, there are hardly any streets, only impenetrable jungle, endless steppe, huge swamps and rough mountains. The native people who could be working as guides and catchers are very often not too enthusiastic to guide the foreign "doctors" on their trips exploring regions where no native would go to voluntarily.

The native catchers, like the Indios living at the Amazon river, do have their homes directly at the place where they also work. They catch fishes from these 'home waters' mainly for eating purposes, but the ornamental fishes sold to exporters also come from these waters; the traders ship the 'precious' small fishes to larger towns where they packed up for their way to our aquaria.

When scientists do discover a new, exciting species, the native fishermen of course leave the security of their well-known home waters and go to the distant places where they catch the fishes that are so precious to us and that bring the natives a much higher profit than the 'old' well-known ones.

It sounds almost too simple, but this is the way how new, exciting species come into the shops and our aquaria. Basically, catching ornamental fishes is the only source of income (in terms of money) for the Indios - and today, even people living in the jungle do need money every now and then.

In South America, the only alternative for natives to catching fishes is to become either a woodcutter or a gold-hunter. Reports by aquarists who have travelled to the South American tropics and have seen the areas where trees are cut down or metals are mined completely uncontrolled are devastating.

Through clearing, the soil that is poor in humus anyway, turns into desert.

The water used for washing gold contains highly toxic substances like, for example, mercury and, as it is not treated before introduced into the rivers, pollutes these rivers so much that these biotopes (and sometimes whole river systems) are very often near to an ecological catastrophe.

In these regions, it is pure nonsense to look for new species: In a few years time, these highly polluted biotopes are probably completely "dead".

Basics:
Where do the 'new' species come from and how do they reach us?

Arrival at the Rhein-Main airport in Frankfurt. Here we see a large pallet with some 150 styrofoam boxes of live tropical fish.

In accordance with the JATA regulations they are well-packed and, in addition, covered with an insulating mat.

Photo: U. Glaser sen.

Political instability and repeated military conflicts especially in the tropical regions of the world we are talking about are two other obstacles for the continuous and secure export of ornamental fishes.

For foreign aquarists or scientists, it is, of course, even more problematic and dangerous to undertake excursions to these areas than for the natives.

Think, for example, of the tropical countries of Africa like Congo, Nigeria or Ghana. Although these countries are repeatedly shaken by political disturbances and military conflicts, people succeed somehow to keep up 'peaceful' businesses and export fishes to Europe.

A similar thing can be said about several South American countries. An innocent fish collector can easily get in between the front lines of a drug war between rivalling drug bosses. To be taken for a messenger of the 'enemy' can be deadly.

Another example is Papua New Guinea. Although we think we know that the natives are no longer man-eaters, it might become rather unpleasant to accidentally pop up in the middle of a tribal war. Also, the rumour that the rich industrial nations pay a lot of money for hostages has spread even in the remotest parts of the world.

Summing up all the dangers and obstacles listed above, it appears even more miraculous how many new species reach us every year.

On the other hand, these obstacles might guarantee that for at least the next twenty years new species and varieties will be discovered and exported for the aquarium hobby.

Adding to the mentioned problems are the difficulties of animal-friendly transport.

To reach far away countries via plane is getting easier, cheaper and faster by the minute, but most of the time, the highly frequented destination airports are those that are attractive for tourists.

Therefore, a freight of 20 000 kg live ornamental fish (including the water) is not so rare on a jumbo jet from Singapore.

But transports from the export centres of the ornamental fish trade, like Manaus, Belem, Santarem, Georgetown (Guyana), Trinidad (Bolivia), Iquitos (Peru) or Lagos (Nigeria), Acra (Ghana), Kinshasa (Congo) are becoming more and more irregular, at least to Europe. I'd like to take the opportunity to thank all the busy exporters and importers who (together with reliant airlines) successfully bring the precious fishes to our aquaria, fast and careful, with as little stress for the animals as possible.

Basics:
Are the native biotopes being 'overfished'?

This unspoiled biotope was photographed in 1991. (Photo- U. Römer)

Sometimes, the aquarium trade is accused of being responsible for fish species becoming extinct through overfishing the natural biotopes. This accusation is simply absurd. As far as food fish are concerned, it is true that the oceans, large lakes and rivers are overfished through the usage of trawls and modern technologies like the sonar that helps to detect large fish swarms in deep waters.

Still, one should also consider the large quantities of industry sewage polluting our waters for being partly responsible for the continuous drop in naturally available food fish. Unfortunately, we know that several countries especially from the Southeast Asian region still practice the catching of seawater fishes for the aquarium hobby with the help of chemical sedatives. European countries have started an initiative to ban all exporters selling fishes caught with this method, a measure we particularly welcome.

Still, this manual is on freshwater fishes in the aquarium hobby. And - to stress this point once again - an overfishing of these fishes in their natural distribution areas is simply not possible. First of all, the fishes are always caught in one single spot; it is absurd to think, a whole river or lake could be emptied this way. Secondly, the fishes are still mainly caught by native Indios who use simple, sometimes self-made nets.

These fishermen never heard of the electronic technologies described above - and in the biotopes they fish in, these technologies couldn't be used anyway.

Finally, one shouldn't forget that the native fishermen do live remotely, far away from our so-called 'civilisation', but this doesn't mean they are stupid or didn't have an insight into certain things.

These people would never put the basis of their daily food and income, the fish, at risk through overfishing the biotopes. We know what we are talking about, we have been there more than once and saw how sensible the Indios are in terms of the quantities they catch.

Further, the governments of these countries do a lot to make sure that laws and quota regulating the fish catching are indeed obeyed; in this respect, the governments are much stricter than we Europeans tend to think.

When talking to people who claim that the aquarium hobby is to be blamed for the drop in naturally occurring fish stocks, one very soon finds out that these people neither really dealt with the topic "aquarium hobby" nor travelled to the places aquarium fishes come from. So, they simply do not know what they are talking about and what reality looks like.

Basics:
Status quo in the native biotopes and the transport of the fishes

The same biotope, now quite ruined, photographed a year later in 1992. (Photo- U. Römer)

Most of the time, these people believe badly investigated reports from the press or television programmes. In both media, journalists are- obviously and unfortunately - forced to produce reports full of "shocking" elements in order to get attention from their audience.

Concluding, we can say that the aquarium trade and hobby are not responsible for the destruction of the fishes' natural biotopes but forest clearing, industrialisation and gold mining, at least in South America.

Here are some figures to illustrate this: An independent scientific study on the tropical Amazon region in Bolivia (Bolivia has the smallest share of tropical Amazon in South America) found out that every year, 50 000 tons of fish can be caught in this area without endangering the natural balance in the biotopes. Of this quantity, so far only 2% are actually made use of, and of these 2%, 99 % are food fish any only 1% ornamental fish!

A report from 1993 by the "Washington Worldwatch Institute" states on the devastating effects of gold mining on nature as follows: Soil and waters are increasingly polluted by mercury and cyanide.

In Brazil alone, about 100 tons mercury pollute the eco-system of the Amazon river.

Mercury is not naturally decomposable. The reports says that probably no other human activity in this region is as destructive as the gold mining.

An estimated 600 million tons of debris are left each year. Up to one million gold-hunters invaded the area and destroyed nature and the home of the Indios.

As this study was made five years ago, it is very likely that today, the situation is even worse. "Our" ornamental fishes are packed and transported with due care and attention, using insulating boxes that contain the plastic bags filled with good water and sufficient air for the long trip.

This method has turned out to be the most secure and animal-friendly.

For long-distance transports, planes are used, because this way of travelling is the most secure and fast.

Renowned airlines are booked, as these airlines guarantee punctual arrivals at the destination airport. It would be nice if the clearance at the European airports was just as fast. Unfortunately, very often the transfer and clearing of the shipments need much longer than the actual flight.

Basics:
New discoveries and breds

*A fish-breeding farm in
Recife (Brazil).
Photo: U. Glaser sen.*

A fish-breeding farm in Recife (Brazil). Photo: U. Glaser sen.

The previous pages contained a lot of information on the situation in the countries where our ornamental fishes come from, although this topic is actually not closely connected to the contents of this book , the "Fishes of the Year".

Still, I think it is not a bad idea to say some basic things about this issue. It might very well be that a beginner in the aquarium hobby reads this manual and I want to make sure that no-one who is interested in taking up the wonderful hobby is taken aback by false "horror" reports in the media about the aquarium trade.

Fish dealers are, mostly, experienced and enthusiastic aquarists themselves so they will make sure to buy their fishes from importers who treat the animals carefully.

But even if the pet shop dealer is a simple businessman, he will handle the fishes animal-friendly because nobody can run a successful business with sick or dead fish.

In countries where the aquarium hobby is very popular large quantities of fish are imported. Obviously, these large quantities are only partly animals caught in nature. Depending on the country of origin, the imports come from small or large breeding farms.

For a long time, most of the commercially bred fishes exported to countries all over the world came from Singapore and the huge breeding farms in Malaysia.

Today, still many commercial breeds come from Malaysia, but also from Sri Lanka, Indonesia, Vietnam, Hongkong, China, Taiwan, Thailand and other Asian countries.

Israel is another country that has to be included in this list as it has gained a reputation not only for high-quality goldfish and koi, but also for good breeds of many other species.

Also, in several South American countries like Brazil, Venezuela, Colombia and Guyana large breeding farms have been set up. Fishes from these farms are exported to countries all over the world.

In Florida/USA (See the big picture on page 7), there are breeding farms so large that one has to visit them by car. Two "newcomers" on the scene are, on the one hand, African countries like Zimbabwe, Kenya and South Africa, and on the other hand, the countries of the former Eastern Bloc, like the Czech Republic, Slovakia, Poland and Hungary that have gained a reputation for good quality fishes after the "Iron Curtain" had come down.

Basics:
Where do the 'new' breeds come from?

In Russia, for example, almost all known species of *Synodontis*-catfish are commercially bred, a thing that seemed impossible until today.

And last but not least, there are the many German hobby breeders as well as the few commercial ones who produce high-quality fishes. Especially in discus breeding, German breeders have made a mark on the scene because (as far as we are informed) they were the first to succeed in breeding the "King of Fishes" in captivity.

As regards other species, German breeders also have a reputation for breeding only the purest blood lines, thus producing fishes of the highest standard, in colour, form and health.

This is why German high-quality breeds are quite expensive but nevertheless much sought-after by enthusiasts the world over.

Commercial breeds from countries with a rather cold climate are, of course, always more expensive than fishes from tropical countries. There, space, water, heat and food are readily available and almost for free, whereas in European countries, especially water and electricity (for heating) are extremely expensive.

Finally, one has to take into consideration that all large export companies in Germany, Holland and the USA buy fishes from all kinds of countries and nurse them into top-condition before exporting them to fish dealers world-wide.

In East Germany, the aquarium hobby has always been very popular. Consequently, numerous breeders of top-quality fishes were and still are to be found there.

In the GDR (German Democratic Republic), the East German breeders were united, according to the political line of that state, under the name "breeding brigade".

These brigades bred excellent aquarium fishes, although only a very limited range of species as the isolation policy of the GDR prevented the breeders from taking part in the world-wide exchange of new breeding strains and species.

Still, for the breeding brigades the aquarium fish trade was a profitable business because the state-owned sales department guaranteed high fixed prices for the fishes.

The central distribution department in East Berlin, on the other hand, sold the fishes (against all rules of the market) for much lower prices, just to get hold of western currencies.

After the German reunion, hard times came about for the East German breeders. Suddenly, the prices for electricity, water, rent etc. rose rapidly and the prices for the fishes had to be adapted to the prices usual in the trade. Some of the former brigades tried to stay together and keep up with the new condition but failed and broke up.

Others, again, recognised the changes soon enough and reacted accordingly; these breeders have now established themselves successfully on the market in form of wholesalers or large commercial breeding companies.

In Zwickau, for example, Mr Günnel's company represents one of Germany's most modern breeding installations with over 1000 aquaria.

The reward for his effort, persistence and diligence is the repeated success at the important fair AQUARAMA in Singapore where he, for the second time, won a first prize and other awards for his fishes, and this, so to speak, in the "lion's den".

But enough of that: Let's take a look at the fascinating fishes we choose as the "Highlights" of 1997. The most attractive and beautiful ones are once more compiled on the included poster so that you can admire them at a glance. To give this collection some kind of structure, we put them together in groups.

First, we present the "winners" of the AQUARAMA competitions, then follow the barbs, African cichlids, etc. As I already mentioned, the Highlights represent new discoveries, rediscoveries, new varieties and also new breds, regarding form and colouration.

All important characteristics of the fishes and the basic care instructions are given in the captions on the poster, more detailed information follow on the upcoming pages.

Basics:
Breeding farms

First of all, let me say a few words about the AQUARAMA. This international fair takes place in Singapore every two years, either in May or June. Thus, it alternates with the second important fair for pet trade, the INTERZOO at Nürnberg/Germany.

The INTERZOO is a fair exclusively for the trade, that means, there is not even one single day this fair is open for the public. The AQUA-RAMA, on the other hand, has at least one "public day" - the fair's last day is open for everyone who is interested.

Fishes of the year:
AQUARAMA Singapore - The winners

But what is most exciting about the AQUARA-MA is the fish competition that is carried through and that awards the most beautiful or rare fishes exhibited. Besides the competition, the fish exhibition (where ornamental fishes from all over the world are presented) is one of the most popular parts of this fair. Due to the popularity of this exhibition and competition, in other countries, fairs have picked up the concept and carry through similar events. Some of them are listed in the back of this manual, together with the literature references. The last AQUARAMA took place in June 1997 and, not least because of the ornamental fish competition, attracted many people. The fair drew 3407 dealers from 60 countries, 180 convention delegates and 14 633 visitors. The judges at the competition were impressed by the high quality of the entries. One of the judges, Mr John Dawes, said: "As in many past years, many of the fish were of good quality. The high overall number of entries, the obvious (and justified) pride with which the winners receive their prizes, and the crowds that are attracted by the competition, leave me in no doubt that the AQUARAMA Fish Competition is a very important part of the show."

Photo 1:
The "Grant Champion" of the new species (wild-caught) was won by Mr Kenny Yap, Qian Hu Fishfarm Trading, Singapore for the presented **'Upside-down-catfish'** X52270-3 „*Heterobagrus leucophasis*" (Photo : E. Schraml).

Photo 2:
As "Grant Champion" in the discus competition, the **S92928 'Turquoise Diskus'** breeding form of Mr Lee Tong Juan, Singapore, was awarded (Photo : J. Gan).

Photo 3:
In the goldfish competition, the beautiful **X31755-3 "Lionhead Oranda"** by Mr Neo Ser Lok, Labeo Aquarium Co., Singapore, won the "Grand Champion" title (Photo : J. Gan).

The first prize, the "Grant Champion" of the guppies was won by the colour-variety **S64525-3 "Mono-Colour"**, bred by Mr Vibhu Perera, Lumbini Aquarium, Wayamba, Sri Lanka. (see the photo on page 18 and the poster A7 - Photo: J. Gan).

Fishes of the year:
Other novelties

Mr Günnel from Germany won the "Grand Champion" award for the most beautiful tetra (fancy): **S39730-4** *Hyphessobrycon ornatus* "White Backfin" was awarded the first prize (Look at the Poster A4- Photo: F. Teigler/A.C.S.)

Last but not least, Mr Günnel won also (and, after 1995, the second time!) the "Grand Champion" in the category new species (bred in captivity) for his fantastic dwarf cichlid **S03592-4** *Apistogramma hongsloi II* (Poster A1 - Photo: J. Glaser).

At the moment, the guppy, *Poecilia reticulata*, has quite a comeback and returns to the focus of the breeders' attention. Most of the time, the triangle-tailed forms are preferred: they are offered in a whole kaleidoscope of colours.

Still, the more wild form like varieties have their share of fans, too, like the round-tailed variety **S64530-3** "Rio Negro" that is commercially bred by Mr Ralf Paul (Poster B7-Photo - F. Teigler/A.C.S.).

In contrast to the closely related, "true" wild form that requires the highest skills when breeding is attempted the "Rio Negro" is absolutely unproblematic. One only has to provide clean, well-filtered water with stable parameters (i.e. the pH and the hardness of the water should not vary; besides, nearly all water conditions are accepted as long as extreme conditions are avoided).

Like in all livebearers, the guppy requires regular water changes of about 10 to 20% of the tank content per week. Guppies are small fish and therefore should be fed fine food. When you follow these few basic rules, you will certainly enjoy your guppies for a long time. You can also expect well-fed females to bear 15 to 30 young once a month. The babies are raised with Artemia nauplii and very fine dry food.

In the last weeks of 1997, an ornamental form of *Xiphophorus maculatus* was marketed under the name **S92927-4** "Red-black coral". We assume that this variety comes from a South African breeding farm, we are not quite sure (Poster C7- Photo: D. Bork). Owing to its wonderful colouration and the unspoilt, typical platy shape, this fish was included in our list of the "fishes of the year". Keeping and breeding

is similar to the maintenance of other livebearers of the kind. The most important features and care instructions for the fish can be obtained from the captions on the poster.

In Florida (USA), the **S92928-3** "Milk Platy", a new form of the livebearer, was bred at the huge fish farm Ekkwill in Tampa Bay. I think, the name "Cappuccino Platy" would be a better choice to describe the looks of this fish... The Milk Platy will tolerate hard water up to 30 GH and pH 8 as in Tampa Bay the water has these parameters. Apart from that, the fish requires the same maintenance as the livebearers described above (Photo on page 18/ F. Teigler A.C.S.).

From India for a very long time only very few species were available to the aquarium hobby. At least to Europe only the odd shipment with commercial breeds of loaches, catfishes and puffers was sent.

Fortunately, this has changed for the better: Some committed Indian exporters have begun to make more fishes from the Indian subcontinent available to the European hobbyists. Now, the efforts of these exporters bear the first fruits and fishes never seen before in our shops are imported quite regularly.

Among these exciting "news" was, for example, a barb species with the trade name "Red Line Torpedo Fish" **X10280-3** *Barbus densisonii* (DAY, 1895). The fish immediately won the third prize for the best new species (wild caught) at the 1997 AQUARAMA. The barb comes from the south Indian state Kerala and attains about 15-20 cm length. It is an algae-eater that likes medium hard water with a pH between 6.8 and 7.8 and temperatures between 18 and 25°C. The tank should be at least 100 cm long and be covered tightly as this barb, like many of its kind, is a very jumpy fellow.

Another "newcomer" from India is the "Neon Hatchet Fish", **X37975-3** *Chela cachius*. The blue shimmer of this fast swimmer is simply breathtaking. Females can be distinguished by the more rounded belly. This about 10 cm long growing beautiful fish is relatively easy to keep: at temperatures around 22-26°C, pH 6.8-7.8 and on typical omnivore foods (Photo 4 on page 18 - F. Teigler/A.C.S.).

Fishes of the year:
Plate: Huge ornamental fish farms in the USA and Brazil.

Aerial photo: EKWILL WATERLIVE RESOURCES, Gibsonton/Florida   Small Photo: Fish farm at Campo Grande/Brazil

Fishes of the year:
Barbs und Livebearers

X10280-3 Barbus denisonii (Photo 1 - J. Amitava Rao)

Round-tailed guppy S64525-3 Poecilia reticulata "Mono - Colour" (Photo 2 - J. Gan)

S92928-3 Xiphophporus maculatus "Milk-Platy" (Photo 3 - A.C.S.)

X37975-3 Blue Chela Chela cachius, (Photo 4 - A.C.S)

A real oddity among the family of barbs is **X55-3442** *Eirmotus octozona*, SCHULTZ, 1959, the False Barb from Borneo. Whenever I look at this fish, I get a little bit nervous because it always looks as if it didn't get enough food. Of course, this is not the case - it is just their very "personal" look (Poster A2 - F. Teigler/A.C.S.).

The False Barb is a small, delicate fish that rarely grows longer than 5 cm. It should be kept in soft, acidic water (pH 5.8-6.5, 24-26°C). The fish is an omnivore, the males can be distinguished by the more slender body shape and the reddish fins. Unfortunately, the fish has a certain susceptibility to oodinium - we recommend to keep a treatment at hand, like amtra medic 1.

Several *Opsaridium* species that in the past had been assigned to the genus *Barilius* are imported from Africa at the moment. This is why the various beautiful species like the Copper-nosed Barilius and other species of **A50915-3** *Osparidium* sp. come from Ghana to our shops. The peaceful, jumpy swarm fish attain a maximum length of 15 cm and therefore should be kept in large aquaria. They are omnivores, but the diet should include frozen animal foods on a regular basis (Poster B2 - F. Teigler/A.C.S.).

Normal, medium hard water at 22 - 24 ° C and a pH of 6.8 - 7.5 is preferred. The unique, beautiful vertical stripe pattern is only displayed by settled-in specimens so that the beauty of this fish is rarely recognised in the tanks of pet shops.

Fishes of the year:
Barbs and African Cichlids

The **X84335-3** *Rasbora* cf. *merah*, is a new, spectacular and, with a maximum length around 3 cm, small barb that is perfectly suited for small aquaria. Its beautiful colouration (see photo 1) and lively behaviour make it an absolute top-hit for all aquarists.

On the European aquarium fish market, this barb appeared together with imports from Singapore; its exact distribution area and place of collection are unknown. The fish looks very much like *Rasbora maculata**, the Spotted Rasbora, but display an additional spot with a golden seam on the shoulder which is larger than the eye diameter. The males are smaller and slimmer.

The small barbs are omnivores but need very fine food. Maintenance is quite simple, temperatures of 22° C to 25°C and a pH of 6.0 to 7.0 are required. The fish was first described in the international newspaper for hobbyists, the AQUALOGnews.

With the "Blue Harlequin", the breeder succeeded to breed a beautiful new colour variety of **X84230-3** *Rasbora heteromorpha* (see the photo 2). In contrast to the "normal" form, the Red Rasbora, in this fish the red colour has been replaced by blue. The Red Harlequin is one of the evergreens in the aquarium hobby; as regards popularity, its blue cousin will certainly catch up very soon.

Keeping the Harlequins is relatively easy, but one has to remember that this fish has to be kept in a swarm of 10 to 30 animals. All other requirements are like in the original form: 22° C - 25°C water temperature, pH 6 - 7, and foods for omnivores. To feel really well, the fish need an environment densely planted with *Cryptocoryne*.

In the African cichlids, too, some newcomers have appeared on the scene. A short while ago, Mimbon Aquarium , Cologne, imported for the first time a beautiful cichlid called **A47704-3** *Nanochromis consortus* ROBERTS & STEWARD, 1976 (poster/B3 - E. Schraml).

This dwarf cichlid from West Africa has all merits of the genus: small size, interesting behaviour and the most beautiful colours. The fish is cave brooder that lives bottomoriented.

* following KOTTELAT: Boraras

In a community tank, you should keep the fish together with labyrinths or tetras. Soft, slightly acidic water with a pH of 6 - 6.8 is preferred. During the settling-in period, the water should have a high oxygen content.

The following eight *Melanochromis* species are included here because now, all of them are scientifically described (Photos on page 20).

Before, they were only known by their trade names, now they have "real", scientific names, too. Why and how these new scientific descriptions came about, you can read in AQUALOG*news* no. 11.

The first species on the list is **A43973-3** *Melanochromis dialeptos*. Among fans of cichlids from Lake Malawi, the fish is also known as "Dwarf Auratus". Until today, *M. dialeptos* has been found exclusively along the south-eastern coast of the lake, near Masinje.

The name "*dialeptos*" derives from Greek and means "very small" - a commentary on the fish's size (Poster/C8 - E. Schraml).

1 *Here the beautiful **X84335-3** Rasbora cf. merah, Gold-spotrasbora (Photo - D. Bork).*

2 *The blue Rasbora heteromorpha **X84230-3** "Blue Harlequin" (Photo - F. Teigler/A.C.S.)*

Fishes of the year:
African Cichlids

A43972-3 Melanochromis cyaneorhabdos (Photo 1 - E. Schraml)

A43972-3 *Melanochromis cyaneorhabdos* is the new name for the also quite well-known Melanochromis "maingano" (see on the poster B8 - Photo: E. Schraml).

This fish is endemic to Likoma Island. The species looks very similar to *M. johannii*; it can be distinguished from the latter (except from tiny differences in colouration) by the number of gill rakers and number of teeth in one row.

The name "*cyaneorhabdos*" again has a Greek origin and hints at the blue horizontal stripes on the fish's body sides.

A78170-3 Pseudotropheus demasoni (Photo 2 - E. Schraml)

Thirdly, there is **A43974-3** *Melanochromis elastodema*, known under the names *M*. "Red" (RIBBINK) and *M*. sp. "Chisumulu johannii" (KONINGS). Probably SPREINAT's *M. interruptus* from Chisumulu is identical, too.

Originally, the species was endemic to the south-western part of Chisumulu Island, but it was released near Likoma Island (Madimba Bay), at Nikatha Bay and even at Thumbi West.

The fish's name derives from Greek and means "broken stripe"; it refers to the broken stripe pattern in male specimens. In the wild, the species lives mainly on filamentous algae (Poster D8 - Photo A. Spreinat).

Another well-known species is the "Black & White Johannii", that now carries the name **A43988-3** *Melanochromis perileucos*; the name means "white edged" and was chosen in reference to the white margin of the males' dorsal fin (Poster F8 - Photo: A. Spreinat).

The species used to live in the eastern parts of Likoma Island but was later also introduced to Thumbi West and Otter Point. The fish lives on plankton and algae growing in the sandy grounds of the fish's biotopes.

In the close examination of the genus and its scientific description, the authors found out that the fish RIBBINK called *Melanochromis* "Blotch" is actually two different species.

One was called **A43962-3** *Melanochromis baliodigma*, the name meaning "spotted pattern". The second, very similar looking species got the name *Melanochromis xanthodigma* "yellow blotch", referring to the yellow pattern the fish displays. For us hobbyists, the easiest way to distinguish the two is count the number of ocelli in adult males.

Melanochromis baliodigma has two to four yellow ocelli and is endemic to Membe Island (south of Chisumulu), **A43998-3** *Melanochromis xanthadigma* displays five to seven ocelli occurs exclusively in the area around Masinje (Poster H8 - Photo: A. Spreinat).

The species name **A43863-3** *Melanochromis benetos* derives from the Greek word for "blue" and thus keeps the formerly known name: The fish used to be called *Melanochromis* "Blue" (Poster A8 - Photo - A. Spreinat). Depending on the fish's mood, it can appear quite differently in colour, especially male specimens. In courtship colouration, the pattern almost completely vanishes. The species is distributed at Mpanga Rocks near Chilumba and around Likoma Island. The typical biotope of the species is the interface of sand and rocks. The Malawi cichlid probably feeds on whatever is available, but it seems to prefer small fishes.

Fishes of the year:
African and South American Cichlids

In the aquarium hobby, **A43983-3** *Melanochromis lepidiaptes* is probably the best known species of the genus. This popularity is certainly the result of the fish's unusual feeding habits: It feeds on the scales of other fishes.

Melanochromis lepidiaptes is probably the best known species of the genus.

This popularity is certainly the result of the fish's unusual feeding habits: It feeds on the scales of other fishes. The former name *Melanochromis* "lepidophage" also hinted at this eating habit. In the aquarium, it was actually observed that the fish attacks other tank inhabitants and eats their scales - but only when it is kept in swarms. Kept pairwise, the cichlid is the most peaceful fish imaginable. *Melanochromis lepidiaptes* is endemic to Makanjila Point (Poster E8 - Photo E. Schraml).

Everything you need to know about typical features and maintenance of these fishes and other cichlids from the same distribution area can be found in AQUALOG's "African Cichlids - Lake Malawi", a book in which, for the first time ever, all cichlids from Lake Malawi are depicted on over 1 500 colour photographs.

Together with one of the very rare imports from Guinea (Africa) the cichlids came to Germany; every now and then, the beautiful fish can be found in the pet shops. *Hemichromis* spec. "Guinea" **A36166-4** has a fantastic blue pearl pattern all over its head and neck, the rest of the body is of a bright red.

Males attain about 10 to 12 cm length, females about 8 - 9 cm. The fish cannot be claimed to be absolutely peaceful but it not as aggressive as other fishes of the genus *Hemichromis*.

The cichlid is an omnivore, feels well in water with temperatures around 24 - 26°C and pH 6.5 - 7.5 and is a pretty, easy-going tank inhabitant.The wonderful, only 6 to 7 cm long cichlid is now, fortunately, more frequently available at pet shops.

The blue fish with the zebra pattern carries the name **A78170-3** *Pseudotropheus demasoni*. It only occurs in the rocky reefs near Ndumbi Point and Pombo Rocks, directly south of the river Ruhuhu. In the wild, the cichlid probably

eats algae and brown algae (see the Photo 2 on page 20). The change to the usual manufactured foods shouldn't pose any problem to its keeper; the fish available at the shops are probably commercial breeds anyway.

A36166-4
Guinea jewel cichlid,
Hemichromis sp.
"Guinea"
(Photo 1 - A.C.S.)

Except the typical "Malawi-water" (i.e. hard, 23° - 25°C and pH 7.5 - 8.5), the fish has no special requirements.

From Congo (Africa), a new, strange cichlid came to our tanks: **A90310-3** *Teleogramma depressum* that has the trade name "Flathead Teleogramma". In contrast to other *Teleogramma* species, this fish has a very flat head; its body width is three times its height. The habitat of this cichlid are the rapids of the river Zaire near the town of Inga. It requires softer water than the Malawi cichlids, with a pH of 6.8 to 7.5 and temperatures between 25° and 28° C. The Flathead Teleogramma is an omnivorous fish.

A90310-3 A splendidly-coloured Teleogramma depressum female
(Photo 2 - F. Warzel)

Fishes of the year:
South American Cichlids

Photo 1: **S72055-3**
Pterophyllum scalare.,
cultivated form "Ghost"
(Photo 1 - F.Teigler /
A.C.S.)

Photo 2: **S99760-4**
Uaru fernandezyepesi
(Photo - F. Warzel)

Photo 3: **S85340-4:**
Satanoperca sp. „Jaru",
the Rio Jaru devil-fish
(Photo - U. Werner)

In some of the new breeds that come to our attention one can argue whether the result is beautiful or ugly; it depends on the personal taste of the onlooker.

This is also true for the new breeding form of **S72055-3** *Pterophyllum scalare*, the "Ghost Angelfish". The transparency of the fish reminds of the famous glassfish. The organs and the skeleton can be seen very well when the fish is lit from behind.

Another typical feature are the blood red gills under the transparent opercles. The care of the Ghost Angelfish is like in all angels: quiet tankmates, subdued lighting, dense plants.

Soft, slightly acidic water (pH 6 - 6.8) stimulates the growth of the animals; specimens kept under these conditions grow faster and larger than angels kept in hard, alkaline water.

When kept in groups, angelfish (like all cichlids) have a distinctive hierarchy. Therefore, you should always buy several young specimens; this way, the hierarchy can establish naturally. If you put together two adult specimens they could turn out to be quarrelsome.

A new eartheater comes from Brazil, more exactly from the Rio Jaru. And that's where the fish got its name from: "Rio Jaru Demonfish".

The pretty **S85340-4** *Satanoperca* sp. "Jaru" grows quite large with an expected maximum size of 20 cm, but in a spacious tank it is easy to keep. The omnivore needs soft water with pH 6 to 7 and temperature 24 to 27°C. It should be kept in a species tank.

The "Venezuelan Triangle Cichlid", *Uaru fernandezyepesi*, **S99760-4** STAWIKOWSKI, 1989, comes from the upper Orinoco system at the Venezuelan/Colombian border.

As you can see experienced hobbyists (see photo 2 and poster F3, Photo: F. Warzel).

The new dwarf cichlid called *Apistogramma* sp. "Pandurini" is quite closely related to *Apistogramma nijsseni*. A short while ago, the fish was scientifically described by RÖMER as *Apistogramma panduro*.

The fish can be distinguished from the already known one by shape and colour of the caudal fin and shape of the mouth and head. This fantastic new species was discovered in Peru. Now, already commercial breeds are available at the shops.

For more information , please read the breeding report in the first issue of the international newspaper AQUALOG*news.* Care is like in all other South American dwarf cichlids: soft water, pH 5.8 to 6.5 and live or frozen food (see the big photo on page 2/3 - D. Bork).

Fishes of the year:
South American Dwarf Cichlids

High-quality breeds of the **S03337-3** "Santarem Black/Red Agassizi" are now available. *Apistogramma agassizi* (Steindachner, 1875) is a fantastic, beautifully coloured fish (Photo 2); the bright colouration is not the result of some breeder's efforts but 100% nature!

The photo of the wild caught specimen on the accompanying poster proofs that the breeds available are no commercially bred colour variety. The photographed fish were caught in the Rio Tapajos near Santarem in Brazil. This fish definitely demonstrates how variable the species *Apistogramma agassizi* is.

Maintenance is the same as in the species described above. By the way: If you want to find all South American dwarf cichlids in one comprehensive book, we recommend AQUALOG "South American Cichlids II" with more than 550 colour photographs.

A really "brand new" import came to our tanks just recently: a dwarf cichlid from Rio Jurua in Peru. This wonderful fish is offered under the trade name **S09898-3** *"Apistogramma Jurua II"*.

The beautiful dwarf cichlid will certainly be successfully bred in captivity and then offered as high-quality breeds in the shops. This fish will definitely enrich our tank life! Care is the same as in all other South American dwarf cichlids. From the tropical parts of Bolivia, the lower Rio Marmore (the big river that forms the border of Bolivia and Brazil) comes the **S03901** *Apistogramma* sp. "Marmore". This cichlid is closely related to *Apistogramma trifasciatus*. Some specimens bred commercially display a deep red dorsal fin that makes the fish especially attractive. Care as in all other *Apistogramma* (Photo 4 - D. Bork).

Another new dwarf cichlid comes from Peru, more exactly, the central part of the Rio Ucayali. *Apistogramma* sp. aff. *payaminonis*, the "Sunset Apistogramma", caused some irritation at first: Its discoverers thought it to be the "real" *Apistogramma payaminonsis*. Meanwhile, it has turned out that the "Sunset Apistogramma" is indeed a new species; it was described by Römer as *Apistogramma atahualpa:* **S03775-3**.

A short time ago, the "real" **S03774** (no picture) *Apistogramma payaminonsis* was caught by Dr. Wolfgang STAECK who managed to bring several live specimens to Germany. The "real one" is not as colourful as its lookalike, the "Sunset". Nevertheless, we show you soon a picture of the original as a supplement in the AQUALOGnews for AQUALOG " South American Cichlids II ". *Apistogramma payaminonsis* requires the same care as all other Apistogrammas (Photo 1 - U. Römer).

Photo 1: **S03775-3** *Apistogramma atahualpa (Photo - U. Römer)*

Photo 2: **S03337-3** *Apistgramma aggassizii "Santarem", the "Santarem Aggy" (Photo - D. Bork)*

S09898 *Apistogramma sp. „Jurua II" (Photo 3 - D. Bork)*

S03901 *Apistogramma sp. "Marmore" , the Mamore dwarf cichlid (Photo 4 - D. Bork)*

Fishes of the year:
South American Catfishes

S19801-3
Corydoras sp. aff.
reynoldsi
(both Photos by D. Bork)
Photo 1: male
Photo 2: pair

Especially in plated or armoured catfishes (*Corydoras* - species), every year new species are discovered or "old" forgotten ones re-discovered. The most attractive ones are introduced on the following pages.

In Brazil, to more be exact, in a sidearm of the Rio Doce in the state Espirito Santo/Bahia, a beautiful small dwarf cat was discovered. It got the trade name **S06165-3** "Bahia dwarf cat" (Photo 3 - H.G. Evers).

S06165-3 Photo 3:
Aspidoras virgulatus
Bahia dwarf catfish,
(Photo - H. G. Evers)

Already in 1980, ISBRÜCKER & NIJSSEN described the species as *Aspidoras virgulatus,* but until recently, the fish was not available for the aquarium hobby. Due to its very small size (4 cm), this cat is also well suited for small tanks. Keeping this omnivorous "cleaning machine" is easy: soft to medium hard water with pH 6.5 - 7.2. A "long-snouted" *Corydoras* species was imported from Peru; the streamlined-like band on the body sides makes **S19412-3** *Corydoras cf. narcissus* II very attractive. Aquarists - and especially all cory-fans - are enthusiastic about this catfish.

S19412-3 Photo 4:
Corydoras cf. narcissus II,
(Photo - F. Schäfer/A.C.S.)

Tending is easy, like in the catfish above. A detailed report by Erwin SCHRAML about certain *Corydoras,* and especially the long-snouted ones is in the first issue of AQUALOG*news*. All known plated catfishes are shown in the AQUALOG "All Corydoras" in over 650 photographs (photo 4 - F. Schäfer/A.C.S.).

For the first time available to hobbyists is the wonderful "Asher Cory", **S19801-3** *Corydoras sp. aff. reynoldsi.* The first to present a picture of this exciting cat was the Japanese magazine "Aquamagazine" that shot the photo at an export station in Manaus. The trade name was lend from the first name of the owner of the huge wholesale company "Turquoise Aquarium": *Corydoras* sp. "Asher". This fish belongs to the group of *Corydoras* with a small, rounded head, like, for example *Corydoras armatus* (**S 18395-3**), *Corydoras osteocarus* (S 19555-3) or *Corydoras loretoensis* (S 19175-3). Except from the typically shaped head, these species have a relatively high dorsal fin which makes them really attractive. Males and females can be easily distinguished, as you can see on the accompanying photographs. These corys are lively, robust fish that need the same care as all corys. If you want to know more about this *Corydoras*, please read the report in AQUALOG*news* no 13. Last year, many of the so-called L-numbers were imported, too. Among these "new" cats, many "mousy" ones and also several already known ones could be found, so that these imports were not as exciting as, for example, those of new cichlids. Still, some beautiful new specimens are now available, and they are presented to you on the next page. If you want to have photos of all known loricariids, check out AQUALOG's "all L-numbers" and the supplements and stickups with the latest discoveries.

Fishes of the year:
South American Catfishes

An outstanding specimen is the **S43432-3** L 228 "Yavari - Lasiancistrus", a black fish with a beautiful white spot pattern. This cat is endemic to Brazil and was caught in the Rio Yavari near the border to Peru. The fish grows only about 10 cm long which makes it suitable for medium-sized aquaria.

The Yavari - Lasiancistrus feels well in soft water with an pH between 5.8 and 6.5. It is an omnivore and good algae-eater, but it is important to provide soft wood for rasping and additional vegetable food (Photo 1)

The L 114 "Orange-Trim Sucker Catfish", **S43114a-3** *Pseudacanthicus* cf. *leopardus*, has been known and popular in the hobby for quite a while. This fascinating catfish can sometimes be found at pet shops, but the colour variety shown here, with the wonderful orange caudal fin, is certainly very rare (see the Photo 2).This sucker cat, like many others of its family, is a very variable species. If all varieties in pattern and colouration would be the basis of assigning an "L-number" (a thing that happened, unfortunately, quite often in the past) we would know more than 1000 different L-numbers by now.

The L114a "Full Orangetail Leopardus" is very rare and thus, when available, very expensive. The fish can attain lengths between 25 cm and 30 cm and is a good choice for a large Amazon tank. In care, the only difference to the previously described species is the need for additional animal (frozen) food.

In the so-called "L-numbers", continuously new L-numbers are created; last year alone, 30 new L-numbers appeared on the scene and there's no end in sight.

Looking at all the "new" L-numbers, one cannot help but think that one or the other fish looks very familiar. One of the fish that is indeed "new" and doesn't fit into this scheme of repeatedly labelling already known fish is the **S43252-3** L252 "Xingu" from Rio Xingu (Photo 3: E. Schraml).

According to the DATZ, a German aquarium magazine, the species is still unknown. Unfortunately, the magazine does not give any care instructions. Photos of all new L-numbers are available as supplements for AQUA-LOG "all L-numbers", either at well-sorted pet shops or directly at the publisher's.

The aquarium magazine "Das Aquarium" labels new loricariids with so-called LDA-numbers. They also provide, together with the number, exact care instructions and tips for keeping and breeding. This helps interested aquarists very much, definitely more than inexact information like "...some L-cat..." and the importer's address.

Bild 1: **S43228-3** *L 228 „Yavari-Lasiancistrus" (Photo: F. Warzel)*

S43114a-3
L 114a
Pseudacanthicus cf. *leopardus* (Photo- A.C.S.)

S43252-3
L 252 Xingu (Photo 3 -E. Schraml)

Fishes of the year:
South American Catfishes

Photo 1: **S43431-3**   *LDA 031 Panaque albomaculatus (Photo - F. Warzel)*

Photo 2: **S43432-3**   *LDA 032 Ancistrinae gen. sp. (Photo - F. Warzel)*

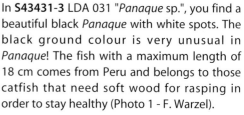

In **S43431-3** LDA 031 "*Panaque* sp.", you find a beautiful black *Panaque* with white spots. The black ground colour is very unusual in *Panaque*! The fish with a maximum length of 18 cm comes from Peru and belongs to those catfish that need soft wood for rasping in order to stay healthy (Photo 1 - F. Warzel).

S43432-3 LDA 032 comes from the Rio Tapajos. There, it was collected by Frank WARZEL who brought it to Germany. This fish is a perfect algae killer and should be fed with food tablets, boiled salad, cucumber etc. (Photo 2 - F. Warzel).

S43433-3 LDA 033 also has the typical rasping mouth. It eats mainly algae, but also other, manufactured foods and soft wood (see on Photo 3 - F. Warzel).

One look at the photos of these three new LDA-numbers is certainly enough to be convinced of the cats' beauty.

Find detailed care instructions for all L- and LDA-numbers in the AQUALOG advisory manual "The most beautiful Loricariids".

Photo 3: **S43433-3**
LDA 033
Baryancistrus sp.
(Photo - F. Warzel)

Fishes of the year:
South American Catfishes

The small sucker cats of the genus *Otocinclus* are known among aquarists as busy, tireless "cleaning women" of their aquaria.

Thus, they lead a rather obscure fish life in our tanks, an unjust fate, at least in the case of *Otocinclus* sp. negros **S55648-3.**

This dwarf is not only nice to look at and a most interesting tank inhabitant, it also is the "world champion" in algae-eating among the *Otocinclus*.

And that's why we christened it "Otto, the nightmare of all algae". (photo: Frank Teigler/A.C.S.).

This ca 3 cm "long" growing, almost black dwarf sucker cat comes from Paraguay. There is no information at all on its breeding habits.

Until now, it has not been scientifically described, but we expect a scientific description to be published in the near future.

Care is easy: temperature 22° - 25°C, soft to medium hard water, pH 6 - 7.5, tablet or dried food and algae. A completely new armoured cat is the beautiful **S02020-3** "Orange-Blackeye Ancistrus". This mutant has an orange body and deep black eyes.

Whether this fish is a natural mutation or a breeding form is not known. The specimens offered at the pet shops are bred by Ralf Paul and other breeders. The body shape of this cat resembles strongly *Ancistrus dolichopterus*.

As regards water, the fish is not very demanding. There is even a breeding report that claims successful propagation at 18° GH and KH and pH 8.5!

The **S02021-3** "Orange-Redeye Ancistrus", on the other hand, is quite well-known in the hobby. It is very probable that this fish is a genuine albino. It is much lighter in colour with the pattern that is known also from all dark *Ancistrus*, still visible.

The animals made their first appearance on the scene in the former GDR and were probably the result of breeding the "normal" *Ancistrus dolichopterus*; we guess the albino form was, first of all, purely accidental.

Another new armoured cat is the **S02022-3** "Orange-Marble Ancistrus".

The breeding specimens are said to be owned by a breeder from the former GDR. Where the fish originally came from , is not known. They could either be a mutation or a cross-breed of different species.

Photo 1: **S55648-3**
Otocinclus sp. "Negros"
(Photo: F. Teigler/A.C.S.)

Photo 2: **S02021-3**
Ancistrus sp. 'Orange Redeye' (Photo: R. Paul)

Photo 3: **S02020-3**
Ancistrus sp.
'Orange blackeye'
(Photo: R. Paul)

Fishes of the year:
South American and Indian Catfishes

Photo 1: **S62305-3**
Planiloricaria cryptodon
*The "Mouthbreeding
Lizard Cat" (Photo - F.
Teigler)*

These interesting *Ancistrus* attain a maximum length of 5 -6 cm in both sexes. At the size of 4 cm, the males display their impressive tentacles. Obviously, the fish are also suited for harder water with a higher pH.

Food requirements are the same as in other *Ancistrus* species. A detailed breeding report about the last three species by breeder Ralf Paul can be read in AQUALOGnews no: 6.

Photo 2: **S92377-3**
Tatia cf. altae
*False-spine Catfish
(Photo - E. Schraml)*

A real sensation comes from the Rio Ucayali basin in Peru: a Spade Cat that is also distributed in Bolivia. **S62305-3** *Planiloricaria cryptodon* (ISBRÜCKER, 1971) can grow as long as 30 cm and its filamentous ray (the "thread" on the

At the moment, the most exciting imports come from Peru because the native exporters are very busy to find new, exciting specimens for our aquaria.

That is why now, species reach us regularly which were very rarely or only accidentally imported in the past.

One of these precious species is the beautiful driftwood cat **S92377-3** *Tatia cf. altae* (FOWLER, 1945). The valid scientific classification is still under discussion. *Tatia altae* was first described in Colombia, whereas this with about 6 cm rather small cat we introduce here comes from Peru (Photo 2 - E. Schraml).

Anyway, this pretty fish will certainly become one of the evergreens in enthusiasts' tanks although its nocturnal lifestyle makes it "invisible" during the day in a community tank.

We recommend to keep it in a South American jungle tank with subdued, "twilight"-like lighting. Keep the cat at 25° - 28°C, pH 5.8 - 6.5 and frozen animal food.

From India, the Indian Frogmouth Cat, **X35505-3** *Chaca chaca*, is imported. The fish has been known for a very long time, but it is rarely found in aquaria (Photo 3 - E. Schraml).

Photo 3: **X35505-3**
Chaca chaca
*Frogmouth catfish
(Photo - E. Schraml)*

upper edge of its tail) can reach the same length. In breeding, the males keep the disc-shaped spawn in their lower lip (Photo 1 - F. Teigler/A.C.S.)!

These interesting cats can only be recommended to experienced aquarists. Still, when kept in a spacious Amazon tank with soft water, pH 5.8 to 6.5 and fed with tablet and frozen food, this cat brings long-lasting joy.

You cannot keep this bizarre, about 20 cm long growing fish in community with small fishes because small fish would be regarded as food, but it is no problem to keep the Frogmouth cat together with larger species - despite its "dangerous" looks, this fish is absolutely peaceful.

It takes frozen as well as tablet food and needs soft to medium hard water, 22° - 25°C and pH 6.5 - 7.8.

Fishes of the year:
Catfishes and other new and rare

The omnivore poses no care problems on its keeper: it thrives on additional frozen food and at pH 6.8 - 8. I think, every aquarist knows the Clown Loach, *Botia macracantha*, a fish that really stands out with its wonderful bright colouration. Still, there is one disadvantage: the fish grows to a maximum size of 30 cm and is thus not suited for smaller aquaria.

Another fish from the family, the **X27755-3**, *Botia striata*, (Photo 2) reaches only 10 cm length and is almost as colourful and decorative, as you can see on the photo on page.

A84780-3 *Synodontis flavitaeniatus*, the Striped Synodontis, (Photo 1) comes from the Congo region in Africa. This fish is an old friend of catfish lovers. In the past, hobbyists had to "rely" on the rather irregular imports from the politically unstable region this fish is endemic to. Today, the Striped *Synodontis* is commercially bred; especially in Russia, several *Synodontis*-species, like *S. decorus*, *S. nigriventris*, *S. brichardi* and others have been bred successfully. Now, beautiful specimens of *S. flavitaeniatus*, the most colourful of all *Synodontis*, are also regularly available. The only species that has not yet been successfully bred in captivity is *Synodontis angelicus*, the Polkadot *Synodontis*, maybe like some other species, this fish breeds like a "cuckoo", that means, it tries to foist its fertilised eggs on a certain mouthbrooding cichlid. Unfortunately, all attempts to find out which cichlid species is actually the right one, have failed. (I think, this is a perfect example for how interesting and exciting the breeding of aquarium fishes is !)

The Striped *Synodontis* reaches up to 20 cm length and is very well suited for community tanks with larger African cichlids and tetras.

The same is true for **X27175-3** *Botia histrionicus* (Photo 3), a beautiful new species that grows only 8 - 10 cm long; the two latter species are regularly available and definitely an alternative to their large relative. Both "small" species are kept in soft to medium hard water at pH 6.8 to 7.8. They are omnivores, additional frozen food is recommended.

Probably for the first time, **X42055-3**, *Crossostoma stigmata*,(Photo 4) has been imported from China. This small, about 6 cm long fish displays a funny behaviour and feeds on everything that grows on surfaces.

Another alleged first import from China is **X57195-3** *Liobagrus* sp., This fish belongs to a rather odd family that includes only nine species. The peculiar animals seems to grow not larger than 10 cm. One should never touch this fish with bare hands: the fin spines are wenomon (Photo 5). And another beautiful wild-caught from China: **X62005-3** *Micronemacheilus pulcher*. With an adult size of 8 cm it is a good choice for aquaria, although this fish is a little bit more sensitive than the other two "Chinamen" (Photo 6).

*Photo 1:**A84780-3** Synodontis flavitaeniatus (Photo - F. Teigler/A.C.S.)*

*Photo 2: **X27755-3** Botia striata (Photo - F. Teigler)*

*Bild 3: **X27175-3** Botia histrionicus (Photo- F. Teigler)/A.C.S.)*

*Photo 4: **X42055-3** Crossostoma stigmata (Photo - E. Schraml)*

*Photo 5: **X57195-3** Liobagrus sp. "China" (Photo - E. Schraml)*

*Photo 6: **X62005-3** Micronemacheilus pulcher (Photo - F. Teigler)*

Fishes of the year:
Mormyrids and other new and rare species

From Africa, the strangely looking, but highly interesting *Campylomormyros rhynchopterus*, **A17664-3** the Snorkel Elephant Fish, is imported. This animals belongs to the family of intelligent elephant fish. The bizarre, about 15 to 20 cm long growing fish is one of the "champions" from this special group of fishes, due to its extremely long trunk(Poster D5).

The Snorkel Elephant Fish needs 24 to 28°C warm, soft water with pH 5.8 to 6.5 and feeds on live food. We recommend this fish only to experienced aquarists.

The best known species from the group of mormyrids is probably Peter's Elephantnose, *Gnathonemus petersi*. Sometimes the variety, **A34101-3** *Gnathonemus petersi* "gold", the Golden Elephantnose, can be found among other imported fishes. For comparison, we show you both Elephantnoses in one photo; the "normal" one is the fish in the background (see on poster E5).

The fish with the name "Henry's Mormyrid" belongs indeed to the mormyrid family, although it looks completely different. **A48730-3** *Isichthys henryi* is very quarrelsome with other fish of its kind. Like in other mormyrids, one should either keep a solitary specimen or not less than five together. Keeping them in community with other, fast fishes, the mormyrids could starve because they are very slow eaters. To sum up: the mormyrids are fishes that should be kept only by experienced hobbyists (Poster F5).

A62120-3 *Pollimyrus nigripinnis*, the Dusky Whale, is another fish from the group of mormyrids. It comes from the central Zaire basin, grows 10 - 12 cm long and is a little bit easier to handle than its relatives above. This fish requires soft water, pH 5.8 to 6.5 and the different available frozen mosquito larvae as a daily diet. We do not claim the species name to be correct - only of very few mormyrids, the live colouration is actually known (Poster G5).

A little sensation is the (alleged) first import of the Peru Toadfish **S28400-3**. These strangely looking animals grow to about 10 cm maximum length and belong to the family Batrachoididae. A short while ago, *Potamobatrachus trispinosus* from South America (Poster H5) was scientifically described for the first time, but the latter is not identical with "our" fish. This Peruvian Toadfish belongs more likely to the genus *Daector* which it resembles very much. Being a predator, it has to be fed live food fish; being more on the leisurely side (characterwise), the food fish for Toadfishes should be rather slow swimmers.

An interesting brackish water species reached us from India: the Spotted Moray Eel. This beautifully patterned fish **X48910-3** has actually two scientific names: in India, it is called *Lycodontus tile*, in Europe *Gymnothorax tile* (Hamilton, 1822). Which genus name is actually the correct one, cannot be decided by us. Every now and then, it is even offered at pet shops.

In the aquarium, Moray Eels can get very old, often 15 to 20 years! During the settling-in period, the fish need to be closely observed because they are slow eaters and very shy. Probably the best way to make Moray Eels feel comfortable in their new home is to keep them in a separate tank until they take their food eagerly. Recommended food are (frozen) shrimps. It is very important to know that in nature, only the young fish live permanently in brackish water while the adults at times leave the brackish waters to live in the sea. Applied to the aquatic hobby, this behaviour calls for thoughtful use of sea salt in the water (common table salt is not enough!). With the fish growing up. you should slowly raise the percentage of sea salt in the water, using 0.5 to 0.8% for young fish and 1.5 to 2% for adult fish. All things considered, I recommend this species only to experienced hobbyists.

Another brackish water species from India is the Indian Snapper, **X57550-3** *Lutjanus* sp. Unfortunately, we cannot give you the full scientific name - we don't know it!

One has to expect the fish to grow about 25 to 30 cm long, so that one can only keep 2 or 3 specimens at a time, unless one owns a gigantic tank. Snappers are quite aggressive among each other, even as young fish, so please provide many hiding places. They are quite intelligent fish and after a short while, they become very friendly towards their owner. When it comes to feeding, you have to offer them "real stuff" - any kind of dry food will be despised (Photo 1 on page 31).

Fishes of the year:
Mormyrids and other new and rare species

The **X89205-2** Aerial Fish, *Sillaginopsis panijus*, is also a species living in brackish water.

With a maximum length of about 40 cm, this fish is hardly suited for aquarium keeping, except one keeps it in a huge exhibition tank.

Anyway, as this fish is so exceptional and "new", we thought it proper to include it here. And - there are aquarists who do own such huge tanks! (see the Photo 2 - F. Teigler/A.C.S.).

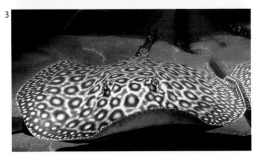

Only to lovers of predators, the Freshwater Gar, **X97105-3** *Xenentodon cancila*, can be recommended. This fish is quick as lightning, looks very elegant and can reach a maximum length of 30 cm. At 12 to 15 cm, it is sexually mature.

The Freshwater Gar feeds on small fishes, specimens accustomed to the aquarium take also frozen food. The distinguishing mark for the different sexes of this egg-laying fish is the black margin of the male's dorsal and anal fin

(Poster G6 - Photo F. Teigler/A.C.S.). Freshly imported from India: the about 20 cm long Striped Peacock Eel, **X57875-3** *Macrognathus* sp. This new fish is a nice alternative to the already known Macrognathus aculeatus (Poster F6 - Photo F. Teigler/A.C.S.).

In Germany, this next fish is called "Swimming Pea" (Poster G7 - Photo F. Teigler/A.C.S.). The Red Green Dwarf Puffer's systematic name, **X91135-3** *Tetraodon (Monotetrus) travancorius* is still being worked on by Dr Ralf BRITZ (Tübingen/Germany).

The dwarfs attain only about 3 cm (females 2 cm), live exclusively in freshwater, do well in medium hard water with pH 6.8 to 7.8 and are fed with (frozen) mosquito larvae.

When you look at the number of various stingrays that are imported right now from the Amazon region for aquarium purposes you can get quite easily confused. Among nearly every single shipping there are specimens that are completely different from known species in colour and pattern. The very attractive stingray we introduce here comes from Peru.

S66047-4 *Potamotrygon* sp. aff. *motoro* is included more frequently than other species and thus offered at pet shops every now and then. Due to its beauty, this fish is very expensive, but we think it is worth its price!

These South American stingrays live in freshwater and need soft, slightly acidic water. The tank for such an animal should be at least 250 cm long and 70 cm deep, the height is not so important; the tank bottom should be covered with very fine sand.

Stingrays are livebearing fish. The sexes can be told apart by the penis-shaped ventral fins that are typical in males. These fish should only be kept by experienced aquarists and in a species tank.

They are very sensitive and easily irritated by other fish. The settling-in period can be positively influenced by feeding worm-like live food that is eaten during the night. Please be extremely careful when you tend your stingray aquarium: the fish never attack but an accidental injury inflicted by the tail sting can be deadly for humans (Poster H7 and photo 3).

X57550-2
Lutjanus spec.
the 'Indian snapper'
(Photo - E. Schraml)

X89205-2
Sillaginopsis panijus,
the 'Indian spiderfish'
(Photo: F. Teigler/A.C.S.)

S66047-4 Potamotrygon
sp. aff. motoro, the
'decorated stingray'
(Photo: E. Schraml)

Fishes of the year:
New and unusual labyrinth fishes and other aquarium occupants

We must not, of course, forget the piranhas. A rare species has recently appeared in the trade, S86610-3, the "vertical-striped piranha", *Serrasalmus humeralis*. This species is relatively peaceful, but unfortunately can grow to 40 cm, a fact which is not obvious from the juveniles (see Poster G2).

They are thus suited only for outsize display aquaria. The "swimming pool" should have a temperature of 24 ° - 28 ° C plus soft water with a pH of 5.8 - 6.5, and bulky foods should be offered.

While we are on the subject of predators, **S00308-3** 'Guyana dogfish', a new South American species should bementioned. This predatory characin, *Acestorhynchus* sp. "Guyana", grows to about 20 cm (Poster F1).

The exact species determination of members of this genus is difficult as regards live specimens. Smaller fishes will be regarded as prey. However, they will live peacefully with larger, quiet, tankmates.

They are easy to maintain given a large aquarium, soft, slightly acid water, plenty of larger frozen foods, and fish of the same size as companions.

A small sensation, in the literal sense of the word, first reached Europe in 1997: **S41820-3**, the "dwarf knife fish", *Hypopygus lepturus*. This, the smallest American knifefish species, grows no larger than 12 cm, and is an absolute asset to the hobby.

These knifefishes should be kept singly or n groups of five or more. They are rather timid at first, but soon become tame and then come out of their hiding-places during the day as well. They are intelligent and entertaining creatures which will give their owner much pleasure.

They should be fed on worms and small dried foods, as they do not have any teeth.

Other data: South American tank, soft water, pH 5.8-6.5. Another true sensation in its day, and still a feast for the eyes, is **X68005-3**, the "thousand dollar fish" from Asia (See the two photos on the poster A5 and B5).

The genus *Chitala*, to which this fish belongs, has shortly been revised, and thereafter it will no longer be known as *Notopterus chitala*, but *Chitala ornata*.

A recent consignment from Asia included a fish with a distinctive coloration and markings. It is probably just a colour variant, as can clearly be seen from the two photos.

This knifefish can attain a size of up to 40 cm, but grows very slowly, and has the ability to adapt to its surroundings. This also means that the onset of sexual maturity is very early.

Neverthless this species is, of course, suited only to very large aquaria, given which it is relatively easy to maintain.

Each individual requires its personal hiding-place, otherwise there will be squabbles. The species has no special water requirements.

This fantastic fish is now bred increasingly fequently; it spawns on stones and roots, and the male guards the eggs. You will find interesting additional information in AQUALOG news No. 6 and No. 14.

The pike cichlids of the genus *Crenicichla* are generally regarded as large, quarrelsome, predators. There are, however, also pretty little dwarf species in the genus, which includes more than 70 described species.

Only recently have we made the acquaintance of **S23460-4**, the Fortaleza dwarf pike cichlid, discovered by Uwe WERNER in Bolivia.

Crenicichla sp.aff. *regani* "Fortaleza" grows to just 10 cm (females only 8 cm), and is thus suited for medium-sized aquaria with a length of 100+ cm.

We will not attempt to describe its splendid coloration here, as Photo E3 on the poster speaks for itself. Maintenance: warm water (25°-27° C South American tank with very soft water and a pH of 5-6.5, frozen (and live) foods (Mosquito larvae, *Mysis, Artemia*, etc).

Successful breeding is likely only given optimal water conditions. See also the report by Uwe WERNER in AQUALOG*news* No. 14.

Fishes of the year:
New and unusual labyrinth fishes and other aquarium occupants

New species are regularly being discovered among the labyrinth fishes as well. Thus although **X14115-3**, the "white-edged red fighting fish, *Betta* sp.aff. *albimarginata* "Pampang", is uncommon, it is already sometimes seen in the trade. You will find a photo of the splendid Pampang dwarf mouthbrooder on the accompanying poster (A6). It comes from Borneo, requires soft water with an acid pH, and a diet of frozen foods. It is best reserved for experienced aquarists.

After a long period of absence, wild specimens of the glorious "Chinese paradise fish", **X58256-3**, are at last coming in again from China. These individuals are very healthy and rather more elongate than those previously seen. It is assumed that this species, *Macropodus ocellatus* (formerly *M.chinensis*) will now become commoner again in the trade as tank-breds as well. They are bubblenest builders, grow to 8 cm long, and do well in moderately hard water with a neutral pH. They are omnivorous, and a diet of frozen foods is advisable. Aquarists wishing to keep these fishes should have some previous experience. (See the photo on the Poster B6).

Not only fishes, but also a few other aquatic creatures make interesting subjects for the aquarium. One example is **A05760-3**, a blue fanshrimp, *Atya* sp. from Africa, more specifically from Cameroon. It is steel-blue and grows to 15 cm.

These shrimps, known in Africa as "Giant African freshwater shrimps", feed on plankton in the wild. In captivity they should be fed tablet and frozen foods. It is not known whether or not they are likely to "chomp" small sleeping fishes as well, but this is a possibility.

They should not be kept with very large fishes, or if they are, then they should at least be provided with plenty of hiding-places in which they can take refuge during and after their moult. After all, shrimp meat is a well-known favourite titbit for many fishes!

The "Australian blue crab", *Cherax tenuimanus*, can grow appreciably larger than its African "colleague". It is bred for food in its native land, but is also an extremely inter-

esting aquarium inmate. An outsized aquarium is required for the purpose, or, even better, a large aquarium with no fishes.

Males and females differ in the size of the claws and the shape of the posterior body; plus in males one pair of abdominal legs have been modified for insemination.

These creatures practise brood care, in that the female carries the eggs and young around on the underside of her abdomen. In order to grow crabs must moult regularly.

After moulting they are soft and defenceless for a time, so they require narrow crevices in which to take refuge.

A crab aquarium must always have substrate. They are easy to maintain: moderately hard to hard water, neutral pH, temperature 15°-14° C.

They are unfussy omnivores which should be given vegetable matter to deter them from attacking plants.

*Bild 1: **S53405-3***
Nannostomus anduzei
(Photo: D. Bork)

*Bild 2: **A05760-3** Atya*
"giant fanshrimp"
(Photo: F. Schäfer A.C.S.)

Fishes of the year:
Crustaceans, killifishes, characins and other new and rare fishes

Shrimps of the genus *Macrobrachium* come to us from Central America, or, like the previous example, from Africa.

In spite of their size (up to 20 cm) and their dangerous "equipment!, they get along together relatively peacefully.

A42855-3, the long-branch shrimp, *Macrobrachium* sp., is no exception. They should not, however, be kept with very small or slow-moving fishes.

Otherwise their maintenance is easy: they have no special water requirements, and, being omnivores, are useful for cleaning up bits of leftover food in the aquarium.

New species of killifishes are also regularly discovered. Thus Dr. Lothar SEEGERS has described the fantastic **A50050** for the first time in AQUALOG "Killifishes of the World: Old World Killis II", as *Nothobranchius fuscotaeniatus* (Poster C6).

This pretty fish from Tanzania, which grows to about 4.5 cm, has now been successfully bred, so that its future in the hobby is hopefully now assured.

They are suitable even for small aquaria, and relatively easy to maintain. Fairly warm (24°-28° C), soft to medium-hard water with a pH of 6.5-7.2 suits them well. A good diet, coupled with additional feeding with the smallest frozen foods, is required.

A quite enchanting dwarf from Australian brackish waters is our next fish, in which males have a bright green-blue back.

The beautiful **X80520-3** "blue-backed rainbowfish", *Pseudomugil cyanodorsalis* Allen SARTL, 1983, was first imported a few years ago, but now these fishes, which attain 3.5 cm, are available in the trade as tank-breds. (see on the Poster D6)

The females are rather colourless; in particular they have no yellow in the fins.

Salt should be added at the rate of about 20 grams (50% cooking salt, 50% sea salt) per hundred litres of water.

This species is suitable only for experienced aquarists. It goes well with other brackish-water dwarfs, for example gobies of the genus *Brachygobius*. A detailed report on the breeding of this species can be found in an issue of AQUALOG*news*.

The majority of the infinitely large characin family are suitable as aquarium fishes, so it comes as no surprise that new species are regularly being discovered, old one re-discovered, and new forms engineered.

Thus we include here **S177240-3**, the "giant splash tetra", *Copella carsevennensis* (REGAN, 1912).

Every aquarist should keep splash tetras at least once. These unique fishes lay hteir eggs out of the water, and the male then uses his large tail to spray the eggs with water until they hatch.

The giant splash tetra comes from French Guiana, whence it is currently being imported in large numbers (for the first time?).

The males attain a length of up to 8 cm (including the long tail), while the females of this very peaceful species remain visibly smaller. They have no special water requirements and are omnivorous.

Another representative of this group is **S17315-3**, the "rainbow copella", *Copella vilmae*.

For a long time this species has for no apparent reason been consigned to the backroom, although it ostensibly has all the prerequisites of a worthwhile aquarium fish, eg interesting behaviour, bright colours, and a bizarre body shape.

These splendid, peaceful ornamental fishes come from the upper Amazon drainage, not far from the town of Tabatinga, and could easily be regularly imported from there.

Unfortunately the demand just hasn't been there so far. These fishes grow to only 6.5 cm, are omnivorous, and are eminently suited to a South American tank containing soft, slightly acid water (see the poster C 4).

Fishes of the year:
Crustaceans, killifishes, characins and other new and rare fishes

Predatory characins are not necessarily popular aquarium fishes.

They often attain the length of a good-sized trout and eventually regard all their tankmates as their personal larder.

This variety, recently imported to Germany for the first time by Aquarium Glaser and found in Peru, is nevertheless so attractive that we can predict it will have some kind of future in the hobby.

The species is **S31705-3**, the "Peruvian predatory characin", *Erythrinus erythrinus* (SCHNEIDER, 1801). At 25 cm it is relatively small, and well suited to appropriately large aquaria with tankmates of the same size.

It is not fussy about water conditions and does well on a diet of frozen "meaty" or live foods. (see the Poster G1).

S39580-4, the blood tetra, *Hyphessobrycon callistus**, is another, this time totally peaceful, characin. Unfortunately it has so far been imported only rarely, although it is found in huge numbers in its native Paraguay.

A cultivated form, known as "callistus minor", is most commonly seen in the trade. These very red tankbreds are sometimes inclined to nip each other's fins, perhaps as the result of inbreeding or inadequate feeding of the young.

These attractive, undemanding, wild fishes from Paraguay grow to only 4-5 cm, and are happy with soft to medium-hard water with a neurtal pH.

They should be well fed on flake and small frozen foods. It is strongly recommended that breeders of blood tetras use them to revitalise their bloodlines. (Poster D4)

One consignment from Brazil included **S48603-3**, the redfin bunny. This small (just 7 cm) fish bears no resemblance to any previously, known description.

Unlike its larger relatives it does not eat plants! However, the shape of the mouth leads us to assume it may be a member of the *Leporellus* genus.

Hence the name: *Leporellus* means "young hare". These attractive fishes will enhance any South American aquarium. They are omnivorous and hence easy to maintain; soft water with a pH of 5.8-6.5 is ideal. (Poster E4)

The ever-popular pencilfishes include the new, just 1.6 cm long, **S53405-3**, the Anduze pencilfish (see Photo 1 on page 33).

It received its name when first described by FERNANDEZ and WEITZMAN, who in 1987 named it *Nannostomus anduzei* in honour of, and gratitude to, Dr Pablo ANDUZE, for his invaluable support during their researches into the fish fauna of southern Venezuela.

Because of its small size, this splendid dwarf is suited to small aquaria with a volume of 10-30 lires.

Until now it has been seen only as a contaminant in shoals of the false neon, *Paracheirodon simulans*, and has thus been generally overlooked.

Now it has been successfully bred, and in consequence is offered in greater numbers in the trade. Given a total hardness of 8-12 dH and a pH of about or slightly less than 7, plus a temperature of about 27° C these pretty little fishes are easy to keep. Because of their small size, suitable foods are fine flake, plus live or frozen *Artemia* nauplii.

All the important data, plus a detailed report on breeding, can be found in the international aquarium newspaper, AQUALOG*news*, No.7. (All issues of the News can be obtained from the publishers of this guide, if unavailable in the trade.)

Occasionally fishes turn up in the trade that are known even to specialist scientists only in ones and twos.

One such species is **S84085-2,** Ogilvie's predator tetra, *Roestes ogilviei* (see Photo 1, page 36). This predatory characin comes from Brazil, and, of course, is suitable only for a suitable single-species aquarium or one containing other fishes of the same general size. But for hobbyists looking for an "oddity", this unique and rare fish is without doubt an interesting and worthwhile choice.

Fishes of the year:
Characins and small cyprinids

labelled "*Astyanax* sp.", but more recently it has been suggested that it may be **S39600-4**, *Hyphessobrycon ecuadoriensis*.

The species is no longer being imported, but good quality tankbreds from a number of breeders are available in the trade. (Poster F4)

It is not only colourful and peaceful, but undemanding in its maintenance. Temperature: 24° - 27° C ; soft to medium-hard water, pH 5.8-7., Omnivore.

A detailed breeding report by Dieter BORK can be found in the magazine 'Das Aquarium', volume 11/95, published by Schmettkamp Verlag/Bornheim.

3 cm long is the maximum size of the fantastic, but sadly rarely seen in the trade, **S06820-3** "Brazilian brilliant tetra", *Axelrodia stigmatias* (FOWLER, 1914) (see Photo 2).

The brilliance of this jewel of nature has to be seen to be believed. If we can only succeed in breeding these dwarfs in sufficient numbers, then there is a place reserved for them high on the ornamental fish popularity scale.

They require soft "amazon-type" water, pH 5.8-6.5, and good quality fine small foods.

S84085-2
Roestes ogilviei,
Ogilvie's predator tetra
(Photo 1: A.C.S.)

S06820-3
Axelrodia stigmatias,
the 'Brazilian brilliant
tetra' (Photo 2: A.C.S.)

S35820-3
Hemigrammus stictus,
the red-tailed tetra
(Photo 3: A.C.S.)

A74063-3
Procatopus nototaenia
"Lutino - Ivory", lampeye
(Photo 4: D. Bork)

Its water requirements present no insoluble difficulties, and if the larger types of frozen food are used there should be no problems with feeding.

That is the great advantage of predators - as a rule they are naturally very hardy and thus easy of maintenance.

A new tetra, well worth considering, whose size and other characteristics seem to have destined it for the hobby, is the "red and blue Colombian".

This splendid little (only 5-6 cm) fish from Colombia (South America) was the 1995 "Fish of the Year", but is nevertheless not as common as it should be in the trade.

Dieter BORK himself caught this fish in the Darien area of Colombia and brought it back to Germany safe and sound. It was originally-

Fishes of the year:
Characins and small cyprinids

A further jewel from the Amazon is the colourful **S35820-3** "red-tailed tetra", *Hemigrammus stictus* (DURBIN, 1909) (see Photo 3, page 36). Wild specimens of this fantastic fish are occasionally found in consignments of cardinals.

As in most *Hemigrammus* the male creates a "mini-territory", so that an aquarium containing a shoal of these fishes offers plenty to watch.

These splendid fishes grow to 4 or 5 cm, like soft water with a slightly acid pH. It is to be hoped that they will soon be bred in quantity.

The cardinal has a cousin in Colombia, **S58206-3**, the Colombian cardinal (Photo 2, page 41). Hardly any aquarium fish is as well-known as the cardinal (*Paracheirodon axelrodi*). No other fish is imported in such large quantites for our hobby.

The articles about it published in the hobby litereature are too numerous to enumerate. Even though it spawns only for those with appropriate experience, the secret of breeding it has been known for many years.

We are well-informed regarding its ecological requirements, and also know the story of how it was discovered. We even know how it got its name, and how it came nowadays to be called *axelrodi* rather than *cardinalis*.

It is also no secret that it is now found not only in the Rio Negro in Brazil, but also in Surinam, Venezuela, and Peru, where it has been introduced, and where stable populations now exist, which are commercially harvested for the ornamental fish trade.

We are also aware that it is also found naturally in Colombia. So can there be anything left to learn about this well-known fish.

Yes, indeed! One small detail has so far been overlooked.

If one keeps Brazilian and Colombian cardinals in the same aquarium, and observes them carefully, then one will notice differences.

The Brazilian form appears more elongate and the blue stripe is brighter behind the adipose fin, the Colombian type is more compressed, the stripe ends before the adipose, and the white of the belly extends further onto the sides. From above the Brazilian cardinal has a narrower dorsal stripe.

The two forms are also different in terms of ultimate size. The Colombian remains visibly smaller (compare photo 2, page 41).

Astoundingly, although a full report on the Colombian locality for the cardinal has been published (BECK, 1994), the author failed to note the differences between the populations.

And photos of perfectly ordinary Brazilian cardinals were used as habitat illustrations in his paper.

In another paper by KOBER (1996), a golden-coloured specimen from Colombia was regarded as an oddity. The saying "can't see the wood for the trees" springs to mind!

Interestingly this paper includes a footnote to the effect that the exporter Willi SCHWARZ observed as long ago as the 1970s that the Colombian cardinal looked different from the Brazilian.

Strangely, until now no-one has investigated the mystery any further. In the hope of clarifying the status of the forms, Erwin SCHRAML sent photos and preserved specimens to Dr. Jacques GERY, the best known expert on tetras.

The reply has come back that there are definitely two morphologically distinct populations, and he is continuing to look into the problem.

The simplest method of establishing the exact status of these populations may be to undertake DNA analyses or to hybridise the forms.

Then, after four generations, it should be possible to establish whether they are subspecies or species in their own right.

So several keen aquarists are being asked to help solve the mystery.

Any volunteers?

Fishes of the year:
Characins and small cyprinids

Other types of "neon tetras" in the trade (see pictorial table on page 41)

Apart from the black and the green neons, which are not true neon tetras (they do not belong to the genus *Paracheirodon*), we know of three species. The first is the long-familiar "ordinary" neon tetra (Photo 1), S58205-3 *Paracheirodon innesi* (MYERS, 1936), which is found chiefly in Peru (Rio Curaray). As one of the most popular of aquarium fishes, it has also been the object of breeders' manipulations. The best known cultivated form is **S58216-3**, the albino neon (photo 4), *Paracheirodon innesi* "albino". Other cultivated forms include **S58220-3**, the brilliant neon tetra (photo 5), which is silver-coloured apart from its bright blue stripe. The third cultivated form is **S58228-3**, the white neon (photo 6), which has simply lost all its colour.

The fourth and smallest species is **S58235-3**, the false neon, *Paracheirodon simulans* (GERY, 1963), which has a relatively extensive natural range and is found in Brazil and Venezuela as well as Colombia. In Colombia it is found together with the introduced form of the cardinal. Specimens with the so-called "gold dust disease" (photo 8, the individual far right) are sometimes imported, particularly from Venezuela. These **58208-3** "gold dust neons" are thus not a true colour variety or a cultivated form. They are quite simply suffering from this harmless gold dust disease, which is also seen in the well-known "gold tetra", *Hemigrammus rodwayi*. This disease poses no threat to health and is caused by a skin reaction. It is found only in wild-caught individuals and cannot be transmitted to other fishes in the aquarium.

Two additional varieties have been bred from the neon tetra. One is **S58245-3**, the diamond headed neon (photo 9), while the other is **S582227**, the veil neon. The latter, however, is no longer available in the trade (hence no photo). It may be that the veil form is difficult or impossible to breed, as in the equivalent form of the White Cloud Mountain minnow, *Tanichthys albonubes* "veil".

All of the neons are shoaling fishes and suited to the aquarium on account of their size (5 - 6 cm). They can easily be fed on good quality flake or small frozen foods. Naturally it is important to note that the ordinary neon and its various cultivated forms are almost always available in the form of hardy tankbreds, which can thus be kept in medium-hard water with a neutral pH.

The cardinal and **S58235-3**, the false neon (*Paracheirodon simulans*) are, on teh other hand, almost invariably wild-caught, and thus require at least an acclimatisation period in soft water with a pH of 5.8-6.5. Our advice is always to buy your fishes, in particular the last two species, only from a dealer you trust.

Be happy to pay a fair, albeit high, price. Always provide living creatures with the special conditions they require; fishes may be newly imported without any period of acclimatization or quarantine, and not acclimated to aquarium water - unfortunately a few irresponsible "pseudo-dealers" do not bother with these essential measures.

If properly maintained cardinals can live to more than 10 years old in the aquarium, although 1-2 years is the norm in the wild.

Happily **S39795-4**, the "gold phantom" or "coffee-bean" tetra, is once again common in the trade. This pretty little tetra received its second common name from breeders in the former East Germany, not on account of its appearance, but because real coffee beans were just as rare there in those bad old days.

This fish was formerly known under the scientific name *Megalamphodus roseus*, but the genus *Megalamphodus* has recently been declared void, and its species placed in *Hyphessobrycon*, so that the correct name is now *Hyphessobrycon roseus*.

Its appearance is very similar to that of the red phantom tetra (*Hyphessobrycon sweglesi*), only it has a yellow rather than red body colour, and less black in the dorsal. This attractive shoaling fish is almost exclusively available as hardy tankbreds, and, given its size of only 3 cm, easy to keep in almost any aquarium. Soft to medium-hard water, a temperature of 23°-27° C, will do fine.

It is an omnivore for which fine flake is adequate, but which appreciates supplementary feeding on small frozen foods.

Fishes of the year:
Characins and small cyprinids

From time to time **S48335-3**, the "Colombian dwarf tetra", *Lebiasina strigata* (see Poster H4) is found as a contaminant in consignments of emperor tetras

In earlier literature this fish has been called the "speckled predator tetra", but that name was inaccurate, as in our experience this fish, which grows to only 6 cm, is exceptionally peaceful towards tankmates. In shape this species closely resembles the pencilfishes (*Nannostomus*); it is easy to keep in soft to medium-hard water with a pH of 6-7, and has no special feeding requirements.

X65505-2, the Chinese sailfin (*Myxocyprinus asiaticus asiaticus*), from northern China, is a sight for sore eyes (see Poster H3). Bred as a food-fish in its native land, in recent years juveniles have found their way into the hobby on account of their fantastic appearance. The species is very easy to keep: omnivorous, temperature 15°-28° C ,neutral pH. The ideal fish, in fact, were it not for its size - it can grow to 60 cm, but adapts readily to its surroundings. Despite its size, its appearance is so beautiful and bizarre that it is recommended for aquarists with very large aquaria.

X28405, the spotted danio (*Brachydanio nigrofasciatus*) (see Poster C2) is back at last, after being lost from the hobby at least 15 years ago. Wild specimens of this jolly little (only 4.5 cm) fish from Burma are coming in via Singapore now and then, and it is to be hoped that they will soon be available again as tank-bred throughout the trade. Maintenance is easy: 24°-28° C , soft or medium-hard water, pH 6-7, the usual good quality dried food.

A11120-3, *Barbus jae*, is a tiny jewel (see Poster D2). In the past this fantastic species has arrived now and then as a contaminant, but invery poor condition, and has thus generally remained unavailable in the trade. Healthy shoals of these colourful, just 2.5-3.5 cm long, barbs are now being imported fairly regularly. Interestingly these shoals often contain numerous individuals with a different appearance: sometimes with additional white spotting, or with a black spot on the dorsal, etc. It would undoubtedly be rewarding to investigate these "variants" (?). The patterns most probably have nothing to do with sexual dimorphism . It is said that males are appreciably more colourful.

Given soft water, pH 5.8-6.5, fine flake and frozen foods, and maintenance presents no special difficulties.

It is sometimes difficult to see why some species, ideally suited to the aquarium and very easy to keep, are for a long time rarely seen in the trade. This is the case with the following two Rasbora species, which are, however, now becoming commoner again.

One is **X84365-3**, the fantastic red-striped Rasbora (*Rasbora pauciperforata*), and the other **X84145-3**, the "ocellated Rasbora" (*Rasbora dorsiocellata*) (see Poster F2). Both come from south-east Asia, are peaceful shoaling fishes, and, above all, the two together make a splendid sight in the aquarium. Both grow to about 5-6.5 cm and are omnivores, and thus easy to feed on good quality flake and frozen foods. They like soft to medium-hard water with a neutral or slightly acid pH. They make no special demands and are rewarding pets.

Known for a long time, but unfortunately still none too common in the trade, are the African lamp-eyes. The majority are ideal for aquarium maintenance. Particularly attractive members of this family include **A74061-3**, the "broad-finned lampeye" (*Procatopus nototaenia*) and **A74020-4**, the colourful "blue-green lampeye" (*Procatopus aberrans*) (photos on page 40).

A brand-new variant of the former (Flaviste/Lutino) has just been imported, which has an ivory-coloured body and black eyes (photo 4, page 36).

It has been possible to import only small individuals of this fish, **A74063-3**, the "ivory Procatopus", but these are now in the hands of good breeders and we can thus assume that they are well on their way to being available as tankbreds from the better dealers.

You will find all the lampeyes in AQUALOG "Old World Killis I". The new form is not at present illustrated, but will be included in the first supplement to the book.

Fishes of the year:
Pictorial table of new and rare species

Photo 1:
S08370-3
Brachyrhamdia sp.,
(Photo: H.G. Evers/A.C.S.)

Photo 2:
X36025-3
Chanda sp.
(Photo: F. Teigler/A.C.S.)

Photo 3:
A74020-4 *Procatopus*
aberrans
(Photo: H.J. Mayland)

Photo 4:
A74061-4 *Procatopus*
nototaenia
(Photo: L. Seegers)

Photo 5: **X37155-3**
Channa bleheri
(Photo: E. Schraml)

Fishes of the year:
Pictorial table of neon tetras

Photo 1: **S58205-3** *Paracheirodon axelrodi from Brazil (Archiv A.C.S.)*
Photo 2: **S58206-3** *Paracheirodon axelrodi from Colombia (E. Schraml)*
Photo 3: **S58215-3** *Paracheirodon innesi Neon Tetra (Archiv A.C.S.)*
Photo 4: **S58216-3** *Paracheirodon innesi 'Albino" Neon Tetra' (D.Bork)*
Photo 5: **S58220-3** *Paracheirodon innesi 'Brillant Neon Tetra' (A.C.S.)*
Photo 6: **S58228-3** *Paracheirodon innesi ' White, Mon Cheri ' (A.C.S.)*
Photo 7: **S58235-3** *Paracheirodon simulans, the false neon (E. Schraml)*
Photo 8: **S58208-3** *Paracheirodon axelrodi 'Golden Dust Cardinal' (A.C.S.)*
Photo 9: **S58245-3** *Paracheirodon innesi 'Diamand-head' (A.C.S.)*

Fishes of the year:
New discoveries, re-discoveries and new tank-breds

An albino form (white with red eyes) of the Lake Malawi ice-blue zebra is now being bred in Taiwan and exported to Europe. **A43625-4**, the "albino Malawi zebra", *Pseudotropheus greshakei* "Albino", like the original form, grows to about 10-13 cm (see Poster C1).

It is omnivorous, requires hard water and an alkaline pH of about 7.5-8.5, and is otherwise easy to maintain. All the cichlids of Lake Malawi, including all the varieties and cultivated forms, are illustrated and described for the first time in the AQUALOG double volume "African Cichlids I & II Malawi". From Brazil comes an interesting catfish, **S49055-3**, "Alexander's broadmouth", *Lophiosilurus alexandri* (see Poster E1).

This bizarre catfish from the Amazon is highly specialised as regards its feeding method. It buries itself in the sandy substrate with only its mouth and "antennae" showing. When an inquisitive small fish investigates the "tentacles", the catfish grabs and swallows the prey as quick as lighting.

It should be obvious from the above that it should be kept only in a species aquarium, or perhaps with large cichlids. As it too can grow very large (30-40 cm), the aquarium must be of suitable size, even though this lurking predator requires little swimming space. "Feeder fishes" should be considered, although it can be accustomed to lumps of fish or other similar items by moving the food to and fro in front of its mouth to be grabbed. This interesting fish has no other special requirements bar soft water with a slightly acid pH.

Also from Brazil is **S08370-3**, the attractive "3-banded imitator catfish", *Brachyrhamdia* sp (photo 1, page 40). This is an as yet undescribed species, but the well-known scientist Dr. ISBRÜCKER is working on a description and name.

The term "imitator catfish" derives from the fact that a few catfishes of this family have modified their appearance to that of armoured catfishes, and juveniles in particular are thus able to find relative safety from enemies among a shoal of Corydoras. The species depicted here is imported mainly with Corydoras sp. "C 22".

It attains a maximum of 7 cm, is totally peaceful, likes soft water with a slightly acid pH, and is thus easy to keep, even in small aquaria.

A new species of freshwater garfish has been imported from one exporter in Recife (Brazil), **S65915-3**, the "red-banded garfish", *Potamorrhapis* sp. (see Poster E6). Unfortunately the exact locality for this species is so far unknown. In contrast to the well-known, rather monochrome, *Potamorrhapis guianensis*, this species has a beautiful red longitudinal band.

It markings cause it somewhat to resemble Menentodon species, but it cannot be connected with that genus as the latter is found only in Asia. This splendid fish is a lurking predator whose arrow-like body shape enables it to dash from cover like a flash of lightning.

Although, like almost all predators, it can adapt its growth to its surroundings, and is also a peaceful e.g. not agressive against fish that are not food for him, it does need a large tank, as it can grow to 30 or 40 cm. It has no special water requirements: relatively soft and slightly acid is, however, best. It requires small feeder fishes during the settling-in period, but can then be "weaned" onto frozen foods.

S11780-4, the "Peruvian orange-tailed suckermouth cat", *Chaetostoma* "Orange-tail (Poster H2) was recently imported from Peru for the first time. These colourful creatures grow to only 8 cm, and sexual dimorphism is apparent as early as 3-4 cm, in that males have a deep orange caudal fin, with the colour subsequently extending onto the posterior part of the body (caudal peduncle) as well. The females, by contrast, have a decorative pattern of spots on the tail.

These fishes are tireless algae-eaters, and thus require vegetarian food. They come from fast-flowing mountain streams, hence although a temperature of 18° - 24° C is apropriate, they require increasingly oxygen-rich water the warmer the temperature.

These attractive suckermouths are bound to win the hearts of aquarists in short order, and will therefore undoubtedly soon be bred in captivity.

Fishes of the year:
New discoveries, re-discoveries and new tank-breds

A very rare dwarf cichlid from Africa is now, we are please to relate, being imported again more regularly from Cameroon: the magnificent **A47703** *Parananochromis caudofasciatus*. This beautiful species remains small at 12 cm, is peaceful, and makes a good tankmate for African characins.

Warning: when maintaing this species ignore the requirements of African cichlids from Lakes Malawi and tanganyika, which like hard alkaline water. *Nanochromis* species come from tropical African rivers and thus must have soft water with a pH of 5.8-6.5 in order to remain in good health and exhibit their full colours as seen in poster C1. Good quality frozen food should be offered.

Glassfishes are widespread in Asia and have long featured in the aquarium. Now there is a new species, **X36025-3**, the "Assam glassfish", *Chanda* sp., from Assam in India. Its shape distinguishes it from other members of its genus - its body is torpedo-shaped, suggesting a fast-swimming hunter, while its "cousins" "hang" peacefully in the water. (Photo on page 40)

It has one advantage over other glassfishes as regards the hobby, namely it does not require any addition of salt to the water (brackish water), but is strictly a freshwater fish. With a size of 6/7 cm it is suitable even for small aquaria. Medium-hard water and a neutral pH are ideal. Supplementary feeding with frozen "live" foods is suggested.

Snakeheads are often regarded rather negatively in the hobby. Not without reason, as they are out-and-out predators. In fact all fishes are predators in principle, and some even eat their own young. But in the case of snakeheads the body form, and in particular the mouth shape, are clear signs of a dangerous hunter.

If they are kept with fish of the same size in a spacious and well-planted aquraium, and, moreover, well fed on the coarser frozen foods, then as a rule nothing untoward will occur.

As luck would have it, one of the most colourful species **X37155-3**, Bleher's snakehead (*Channa bleheri*) from India (photo 5, page 40), is now again commoner in the trade. It is not only the most attractively coloured, but also the least aggressive, member of its genus. The wild specimens which are now and then imported from India are also very expensive.

This is because they are caught under very difficult conditions in Assam, and then have to make a long arduous journey to the exporter In Calcutta. Their maintenance requirements are fairly simple: medium-hard water with a neutral pH.

Only the real cognoscenti in the hobby are aware that Madagascar is home to a number of splendid, colourful fishes, in particular some fantastic cichlids. The island of Madagascar has - not without good reason - imposed a strict ban on the commercial exportation of all wild animals.

However, one off exports of numbers of different species are permitted every few years.

Thus now and then a few of these fishes come into the hands ofskilled breeders. One such is **A54010-4**, the marakely, *Paratilapia bleekeri*.

These fishes grow to 15-18 cm and do not show their fantastic mosaic pattern properly until they are adults, as depicted in Poster photo G3.

As only tankbreds are available in the trade their maintenance is relatively simple.

A large aquarium with medium-hard water and a neutral pH will suffice. They are omnivores which, however, also enjoy good quality frozen foods.

Australia is best known for its colourful rainbowfishes. The most beautiful, **X60325-3**, the Lake Tebera rainbowfish, *Melanotaenia herbertaxelrodi* (see photo 1, page 44), had practically been forgotten as it was no longer being imported, but this beautiful fish is now again available as good quality tankbreds.

These fishes like soft to medium-hard water with a slightly acid pH; they are omnviores and easy to keep.

Fishes of the year:
New discoveries, re-discoveries and new tank-breds

Not only do many lovely rainbowfishes originate from Australia; there is also **X53010-3**, the "Australian cyprigoby" (*Hypselestris compressys*, whose splendid coloration is unequalled (photo 2). There is, of course, a simple reason why this glorious species is so rarely seen in the trade. Only courting males exhibit the fantastic coloration; females and juveniles are rather drab.

It is unfortunate that only what is colourful, sells. That is why we are presenting this fish here. If aquarists were only aware what fantastic fish the grey youngsters turn into, then undoubtedly they would become one of the most popular ornamental fishes.

This goby, which is also found in New Guinea, but available mainly as tankbreds, is relatively easy to keep. It grows to 9-11 cm, and tolerates water temperatures between 10° and 30°C, although these extremes should, of course, be avoided.

During the overwintering phase in nature the minimum temperature can drop to 10° C, while at the other end of the scale the summer maximum is up to 30° C . 22° C is an appropriate happy medium.

The water should be medium-hard to hard and have a neutral pH. They are omnivores, and take frozen foods, with small krill in particular bringing out the best colours and triggering courtship behaviour. As already mentioned, the males are appreciably more colourful. The eggs are laid on leaves and flat stones, and the male guards thebrood.

Yet another African characin is particularly worth mentioning here. **A58210-4**, the attractive "African moon tetra" (*Bathyaethiops caudo- maculatus*) (photo 3). This species was formerly assigned to the genus *Phenacogrammus*. Whether this has caused confusion and thus rendered this species something of a Cinderella in the hobby, who can tell. Be that as it may, although it is seldom imported, it can now be found again in the trade as good quality tankbreds. It grows to just 7-8 cm, does very well in soft or medium-hard water with a pH of 6-7.5, eats anything, and is eminently suitable as atankmate for Congo tetras and other African fishes, for example African dwarf cichlids.

Photo 1:   **X60325-3** *Melanotaenia herbertaxelrodi Lake Tebera*
Photo 2:   **X53010-3** *Hypselestris compressys from Australia*
Photo 3:   **A58210-4** *Bathyaethiops caudomculatus*
           (All photos: A.C.S.)

The AQUALOG System:
Information and exploration

AQUALOG Lexicon

The AQUALOG team has set itself the goal to catalogue all known ornamental fishes of the world - and this task will, of course, take several years, as there are over 40 000 fish species.

Compiling an AQUALOG lexicon, we take a certain group of fishes, label all known species with code-numbers, look for the newest results of fish research about natural distribution, features and maintenance of the fishes and try to get the best photographs, often from the most remote parts of the world.

Our ingenious code-number-system labels every species with its own individual code-number which the fish keeps even if a scientific re-naming occurs.

And not only the species gets a number, also each variety, distinguishing locality, colour, and breeding form.

This system makes every fish absolutely distinct for everybody. With it, international communication is very easy, because a simple number crosses almost all language barriers.

This is an advantage not only for dealers, but for hobbyists, too, and thus for all people involved in the aquarium hobby.

Again and again, new fish species are discovered or new varieties bred. Consequently, the number of fishes assigned to a certain group changes constantly and information from available specialist literature is only reliable within certain time limits. Thus, an identification lexicon that is up-to-date today is outdated after as little as one year.

To give aquarists an identification 'tool' that stays up-to-date for many years, we developed our ingenious patented code-number system.

When going to press, our books contain all fishes that are known to that date. All newly discovered or bred species are regularly published as either supplements or as so-called "stickups" in AQUALOG*news*.

These supplementary peel-back stickers can be attached to the empty pages in the back of the books.

As you can see, we provide the latest information from specialists for hobbyists. Over the years, your AQUALOG books will 'grow' to a complete encyclopaedia on ornamental fishes, a beautiful lexicon that is never outdated and easy to use.

AQUALOG*news*

AQUALOGnews is the first international newspaper for aquarists, published in four-colour print, available in either German or English language and full of the latest news from the aquatic world.

The following rubrics are included:Top Ten, Brand New, Evergreens, Technics, Terraristics, Fish Doctor and Flora. Further, there are travel accounts, breeding reports, stories about new and well-known fish etc.

The news gives us the opportunity to be highly actual, because up to one week before going to press, we can include reports and the 'hottest' available information.

This way, every six weeks a newspaper for friends of the aquarium hobby is published that makes sure to inform you about the latest 'arrivals' waiting for you at your local pet shop.

AQUALOG*news* can be subscribed to and contains 40 supplementary stickers for your AQUALOG books in 12 issues. You can subscribe to the news either via your local pet shop or directly at the publishers.

Issues without stickups (print run: 80 000) are available at well-sorted pet shops. The newspaper also informs you about newly published supplements.

AQUALOG Special

The Specials series is not intended to repeat all the things that were already known twenty years ago, like 'how to build your own aquarium' - something, probably nobody practises anymore, because there is no need to do so.

We provide the latest and most important information on fish keeping and tending in precise and easily understandable language.

We want to offer advice that helps you to avoid mistakes - and your fishes to live a healthy life.

We intend to win more and more friends for our beautiful and healthy (because stress-reducing!) hobby.

Order our new free catalogue, where all our previous and future books are shown and described.

ISBN: 3-931702-49-9

ISBN: 3-931702-41-3

ISBN: 3-931702-39-1

ISBN: 3-931702-34-0

ISBN: 3-931702-43-X

ISBN: 3-931702-53-7

ISBN: 3-931702-45-6

ISBN: 3-931702-51-0

Upcoming specials:

Freshwater Coral Fish: Cichlids from Lake Tanganjika
The Colourful World of Livebearers
Beautiful Tetras I 'Small species'
Beautiful Tetras II 'Big species'
Beloved Monsters: Bizarre Fishes
Odd Shapes (...but they are fish!)
Horror or Passion: The most beautiful Tarantulas
Popular Aquarium Fishes I: Fishes for Beginners
Popular Aquarium Fishes II: Fishes for Advanced
                                            Hobbyists
Popular Aquarium Fishes III: Fishes for Experts

Decorative Aquaria :	A Malawi Biotope Tank
Decorative Aquaria :	A Tanganjika Biotope Tank
Decorative Aquaria :	An Amazonas Biotope Tank
Decorative Aquaria :	A Marine Tank for Beginners
Decorative Aquaria :	A Dutch Waterplant Tank
Decorative Aquaria :	Westafrica Biotope Tank
Decorative Aquaria :	South Asia Biotope Tank
Decorative Aquaria :	Impressive Cichlids from Central America
Decorative Aquaria :	Amazing Dwarf Cichlids from South America
Decorative Aquaria :	An Aquaterrarium

Future Specials

Order your free copy of
AQUALOG*news* and
the A.C.S. programme!

Infos and news:

Verlag A.C.S. GmbH
Liebigstr. 1
D-63110 Rodgau

Tel.: +49 (0) 06106 - 64 46 91
Fax: +49 (0) 06106 - 64 46 92

E-Mail: acs@aqualog.de
http://www.aqualog.de

© Verlag A.C.S. GmbH

Index